Meaning

The Secret of Being Alive

Cliff Havener

Beaver's Pond Press, Inc.

Edina, Minnesota

"People say that what we're all seeking is a meaning for life. I don't think that's what we're really seeking. I think that what we're seeking is an experience of being alive, so that our life experiences on the purely physical plane will have resonance within our own innermost being and reality, so that we actually feel the rapture of being alive."

—Joseph Campbell, *The Power of Myth*,
with Bill Moyers

To Chris and Jeff

Preface

A systems view of life is uncommon at this stage of human evolution. People who have such a view often find themselves isolated from others, even though their greatest strength is their ability to make connections. I was fortunate enough to have a colleague in the creation of this book who also understands systems. She pointed out, for example, the historical events of the sixteenth and seventeenth centuries that created most of the cultural norms we live with today. She saw the basis of dysfunction common to all major social institutions—business, education, government.

Some of her life experiences provided examples I use to illustrate the principles explored here. She found most of the quotes that precede each chapter. She edited and re-edited the manuscript until we were both satisfied. She even selected the graphic for the cover.

Thank you, Margaret Thorpe, for your unlimited commitment, dedication, and talent.

Acknowledgments

M ost authors limit their acknowledgments to the people who helped them write their books. I'd like to extend that to include the people who helped me develop the perspective that is the substance of this book.

My wife, Linda, gave me the opportunity to live "the unity of opposites".

My father championed my existence.

Joe Burke, Gwen Welckle, Tom Eckstein, Doug Shifflet, and Ron Toensing "know". They always supported my search, even when it got precarious. My children, Teri, Rand, and Stacey, inspired it.

A few people made major contributions to the perspective that evolved: George Land and Channing Stowell through our personal association; Abraham Maslow, E. Paul Torrance, and Ludwig von Bertalanffy through their writings.

But the impetus for the journey that produced the perspective came from the many people I met, especially senior managers in corporations. They drove me to ask myself, "How come my best stuff gets me into the most trouble?" They provided a problem worth solving.

I also want to thank those independent professionals who made it not only feasible but vastly preferable for me to publish this book myself. Milt Adams at Beaver's Pond Press provided full-service publishing capabilities through his network of designers, editors, proofreaders, and printers. Jack Caravela at Mori Studio designed the book layout and its cover. Jack was a joy to work with. And after Margaret and I were reading what should be on each page as though it really *were* on the page, Phil Freshman and Steve Waryan applied the final polish.

Contents

Introduction

This is a book about the *Why* of things—that territory of life we're forbidden to enter. I wrote it to show why life is so lifeless for so many people, why meaning has been so difficult to find, and what to do about it if you want to.

Mankind's search for meaning has been a long, frustrating journey that began shortly after the rise of civilization. Now that we are beginning to understand complex systems, we're finding that civilization itself, as we have defined it, is the *major* obstacle to finding meaning in life.

Finding meaning in life requires having a systems view of it, because the things of life *are* systems. We talk about them. We refer to systems of government, systems of communication, ecological systems, systems of business, systems of thinking—but most of us have a linear view, not a systems view, of systems. That's why they have no meaning to us. If you already know what these four sentences really mean, they don't apply to you. Your only reason to read this book would be to find out why you've been called "crazy" a lot and have had such a hard time "fitting in". If your reasons for reading this book are personal, read it as it's written, from this Introduction through to the Conclusion. If your reasons to read this book are related to business, read Chapter Ten first. It'll show you why you should read the first nine chapters.

Many people use the terms *meaning* and *spirituality* interchangeably. They mean *meaningful to me*. Most people are unique individuals, both genetically and due to their experiences—nature *and* nurture. What is meaningful is unique to the individual. But for everyone, the prerequisite to finding what is meaningful is the ability to see meaning—the purpose, the intent behind the things that comprise our lives. Civilization is a normative social system that requires us to ignore that part of reality. Society trains us to be unable to see meaning.

Meaning and spirituality, in the hands of social institutions, look like the traditional practice of medicine—prescriptions written in unintelligible jargon by elitists primarily concerned with gathering power and exercising control over others. Treating meaning and spirituality as mysteries of perpetual confoundment is the mechanism of control. It may well be the ultimate obscenity of the human condition.

This book does not prescribe what is or should be meaningful to anyone. Rather, it provides a perspective that promotes an individual's ability to see meaning and, from that, find what is meaningful to him or her. It provides *tools* of personal freedom.

My own search began in 1973 as a question—"How come my best stuff gets me into the most trouble?" By this time, I'd been working in large corporations—General Foods, M&M/Mars, Pillsbury—for thirteen years. I'd noticed a repeating pattern. Every time I solved a problem of any substance, I found myself in disfavor with management.

I was confused. The solutions were soundly based. They were practical. The logic behind them was self-evident. The cause of the unfavorable reaction was that the solution not only required doing things differently and doing different things, but it also required *seeing* things differently. It required deviating from the status quo. Several times I'd been advised, "You have to work inside their comfort zone." That was nonsense. Somewhere "inside their comfort zone" was the root cause of the problem.

Someone once said, "The height of insanity is doing the same thing, the same way, over and over, and expecting different results." Resolving the root cause of a problem and maintaining the status quo are mutually exclusive. As Albert Einstein once said, "The world will not evolve past its current state of crisis by using the same thinking that created the situation." "Their comfort zone" is "the same thinking that created the situation".

Over the next twenty-five years, I solved the riddle. I found out why my best stuff got me into the most trouble. In the process, I discovered why the meaning of things is so hard to see.

Meaning is no big mystery. When things make no sense, they are meaningless. Many aspects of the human condition are beyond senseless. They are self-contradictory—anti-sense—"Catch 22s". A Catch 22 is not simply a paradox, an apparent contradiction that may actually be true. A Catch 22 *is* self-contradictory—leaping, screaming, pole-vaulting nonsense. Catch 22s raise the possibility that the very idea of meaning may be a myth. Yet, meaning is what affirms to a person that he or she actually exists. Without it, a person lives a purely mechanical existence, going through all the motions of life without feeling alive. In *Flow: The Psychology of Optimal Experience*, Mihaly Csikszentmihalyi called this condition "existential dread, psychic entropy, a fear of being". In *Man's Search for Meaning*, Viktor Frankl called it "the existential vacuum". The common name for it is "the walking dead". It's caused by external dependency.

An externally dependent person is exactly that—dependent on things outside of him or herself to direct his or her life. Externally dependent people don't ask questions. They follow orders. They don't make waves. They are faithful followers, true believers. If they care about meaning at all, they take no responsibility to find it themselves. They seem to believe that the source of whatever direction they're following will explain it to them. In the absence of that explanation, they follow orders "on faith". Their god is "correct and proper form".

There are a few things I'd like to tell you about myself and this book before you read it. I'm an artist by nature and a scientist by training. I spent thirty-eight years in business, primarily involved with creating new businesses, figuring out why a business wasn't working or trying to turn around a dying business. A perpetual "fish out of water" you say? Absolutely. I've lived most of my life outside whatever "comfort zone" I had at the time. Why? Because life's more interesting that way. I've found two very different views of knowledge. One is the open view, that knowledge is a platform for further exploration and growth. Knowing what you know provides self-confidence. It also defines what to learn next. The other is the closed view, that knowledge is protection from real and imagined threats. People wrap their knowledge around themselves. They spend their time dissecting and intensifying it, reinforcing their stockade. This makes knowledge a prison.

Staying inside a safe perimeter, doing the same things over and over, from the same point of view, looks to me to be what Hell is all about. It's terminally boring. Conversely, exploring forced me to realize that while specific details—facts, figures, names, and places change constantly, there are basic principles common to every aspect of life—the principles of systems. *The ability to see systems divulges the meaning of things.*

When some particular thing doesn't work, or looks senseless, we just look at it to find out why. But when we're surrounded by nonsense, we say "it's the system." That's what I did in 1973, when I realized that what I'd been encountering was not unique to the individual companies I'd worked for. It was indigenous to the whole institution of "business". At the time, I didn't know what "the system" meant. I've spent the last twenty-five years correcting that. Part I—"The System", passes along what I've learned. Having a systems view is the critical prerequisite for making sense of things, for having the ability to find their meaning.

Parts I and II are the "what"s and "why"s—the content. Part III—"Changing the System"—is how to use it. It shows how a person can reinvent any system for him or herself so that it has meaning.

Most discussions of meaning and spirituality focus on our personal life, which typically excludes our professional life. What's more personal than our work? It's what we do—our craft—a place where we get to use our unique abilities. Potentially, it's the most direct means we have of affirming our existence, provided we define what we do (internal dependence) instead of letting what we do define us (external dependence). Lack of meaning in our work lives may be more devastating to our sense of being alive than a lack of meaning anywhere else. I challenge the separation of personal and professional life. Our work is our primary art form. That's as personal as it gets.

Many books about meaning and spirituality are metaphorical. By that I mean they describe the human condition symbolically rather than literally. This is typical of theology, mythology, and science fiction. The problem with metaphors is that a person must already have solved the riddle to recognize the metaphor. Metaphors communicate *after* the fact. They're not useful for solving riddles.

This book is about solving the riddle. That's why it doesn't speak in metaphors. It talks directly about meaning, substance, spirituality, and the reasons for their absence. It challenges much of what many people believe. It examines how most of us think and what we think about. It's outside most people's "comfort zone" but much closer to home than many may care to get. Under any circumstances, it demands creative reading.

E. Paul Torrance, who has done landmark research on creativity in the American educational system for more than forty years, talks about creative reading in his book *Why Fly?*:

> When you read, it is important that you think about the many possible uses of the information which you are reading. It is especially important that you think of the various ways in which the information could be used in your personal and professional life. In reading, do not just ask, "What is the author saying?" Also ask, "How can I use what the author is saying?" Do not stop with just one use. Think of as many uses as you can for the important ideas presented. Jot down some of these uses for future reference.

I'd like to add my own thought. Also ask yourself how you feel about what you're reading. Do you agree? Do you disagree? Why? After you've answered the first "why?" ask yourself why you believe that answer. "WHY?" is the question we've been trained not to ask. It opens the door to meaning. I believe that if you don't read this book this way, it will be meaningless to you.

One last thing. If you're reading along and something doesn't register, don't worry about it. This book is not so linear that you won't be able to understand what follows. Besides that, its meaning will show up—probably when you least expect it. The less you grind it around in your head, the faster its meaning will show up. When you get to Chapter Six, you'll see why I'm giving you this advice.

Part I

The System

Systems are the basic structure of everything we live in, of everything that exists—from an atom to our universe, from ourselves as individuals to personal relationships, to societies, to the community of mankind. To find meaning, we need a systems view of our own reality. We're born with this ability, but we've been trained to deny it. Resurrecting it is the first step on any journey toward meaning.

People who, as adults, are innovative, creative, perceptive, or insightful have retained their ability to have a systems view of reality rather than a serial view. Typically, they don't consciously understand why or how it works. They view it as intuitive or instinctive. Most have retained it in spite of substantial attempts to extinguish it. This part of the book lays the foundation for consciously developing a systems view of reality.

The first chapter is about the effects of "the system" in one institution—business. The next two provide the basic principles of systems. The fourth chapter describes the origin and nature of the social system we call the United States of America—a society that prevents most people from finding meaning in their lives.

Part I provides the first set of tools. They identify the principles behind the specific events we experience. The ability to see the principles behind specifics discloses their cause. *The ability to see cause is the ability to find meaning.*

There was only one catch and that was Catch-22, which specified that a concern for one's own safety in the face of dangers that were real and immediate was the process of a rational mind.... Orr would be crazy to fly more missions and sane if he didn't, but if he was sane he had to fly them. If he flew them he was crazy and didn't have to; but if he didn't he was sane and had to.

—Joseph Heller, *Catch-22*

Chapter One
Good Stuff/Big Trouble

From time to time, we smash, face first, into a wall we didn't see, leaving us stunned and muttering, "What the hell was that?" Here are some of the ones I hit that led to the question "How come my best stuff gets me into the most trouble?" They may feel strangely familiar. I have a network of friends who have all had the same experiences, just in different places at different times. This is the stuff of which *Dilbert* is made.

The Dog Food That Dogs Wouldn't Eat (See what I mean?)

In 1966 I'd just become an associate brand manager in General Foods' Post Division, responsible for two dog food products—Gaines™ Meal and Gaines™ Biscuits and Bits. Gaines™ Meal's sales were falling at about the same rate Purina Dog Chow™'s were rising. "Stop the bleeding, stop the bleeding," the company said. The division hired Doyle, Dane, Bernbach, the hottest ad agency in New York at the time, to help. Several runs at a new campaign got so desperate they became bizarre. Finally, the copy chief threw up her hands and screamed, "Of course they're crap! There's nothing to say about this product." She was right.

I'd started at General Foods in research and development for Gaines Dog Foods. I wasn't trained in marketing. My degree was in biochemistry—a major in animal nutrition, a minor in genetics. I think I was the only person in marketing who wasn't an Ivy League M.B.A. I'd gotten into marketing because I'd been successful in Gaines Professional Services—selling Gaines dog foods to veterinarians, breeders, boarding kennels, and humane societies. I'd gotten that job for reasons that made sense. Technically, I knew what to feed dogs. But I also had a kennel of field-trial English setters. I personally experienced all the conditions my customers experienced—growth, maintenance, gestation, lactation. I knew the products and their use—both sides of the business. I could work effectively with customers because I understood them. My move into brand management put a stranger into a strange land.

To turn old dying Gaines™ Meal around, I first asked, "What's causing loss of sales?" The answer: "Dogs won't eat it." A dog would eat Gaines™ Meal if that was all it knew. But once it tasted Purina Dog Chow™, it wouldn't eat Gaines™ Meal again. We had a product that guaranteed brand loyalty to our most direct competitor.

The solution to this problem seemed pretty obvious. I saw it as self-evident truth.

Question: "How do we turn Gaines™ Meal around?"

Answer: "Give the dogs food they like to eat."

This looks pretty basic, doesn't it? What are the odds somebody would *not* agree with it?

Confidently, I called my old boss's boss in R&D.

"How long will it take to get a formula that makes Gaines™ Meal taste as good or better than Purina Dog Chow?™" I asked.

"About ten minutes," he replied.

"Why so long?"

"Well, that's how long it'll take me to dig it out of the file."

"How long has it been in the file?"

"Oh, a couple of years or so."

"How come it's in the file and not the product? This isn't a new problem."

"Yeah, I know," he responded, "but nobody ever asked for it before."

"What the hell?" I thought to myself. "Oh well, maybe my predecessor was an idiot."

He was, but for a good reason. As I was to find out, it was a critical requirement for career advancement.

I put together a $5 million re-introductory plan. In 1966 that was real money. I took it seriously—new product formulation, new product look, new package, new ad campaign, and a trial-inducing promotion program. All of it was for the purpose of saying, "Hey, we finally pulled our head out of our ass. Now your dog will actually eat this stuff."

The division marketing director reviewed the plan. First he said, "This is great. I love it." Then he said, "I have one little issue, but otherwise, let's go."

"What's the little issue?"

"Well, you show a $500,000 increase in the cost of finished goods for the twelve months following re-introduction. Don't do that, but go ahead with the rest of it."

"That's not a little issue," I explained. "That's due to the formula change that makes Gaines™ Meal taste better than Purina Dog Chow™. It's the foundation of the re-introduction. If we don't do that, we have no reason to do the rest."

"Don't you think you're taking this a bit too seriously?" he asked. All I could think of was, *What the...???* All I said was, "No, I don't." I was still assuming that the primary goal was to save a dying business and that the marketing director and I shared it. Maybe not.

I collected myself enough to say, "I'm confused. If you're willing to spend $4,500,000 on the rest of the program, why wouldn't you spend $500,000 on its most critical issue?"

"Well, you know Charlie, the manager of our dog food plant? The plant just installed least cost formulation. His number one MBO is to substitute the lowest-cost raw ingredients, within the nutritional parameters of the formula, to produce finished goods at the lowest possible cost. If you change the formula, you'll hang a $500,000 albatross around his neck." ("MBO" stands for "Management by Objectives," the major management craze of the mid-1960s)

"No, I won't. That MBO applies to existing formulas. If I change a formula, that puts it outside his MBO."

"Technically, you're right," the marketing director replied, "but management won't look at the P&L that closely. They'll just look at total Cost of Goods Sold. He'll be $500,000 less favorable than he could have been."

The longer this conversation lasted, the faster the room spun. I was beginning to understand how Alice felt in Wonderland. Maybe saving the business *wasn't* the primary goal. I had to find out.

"O.K., let me ask you another question. What's my job? Is it to turn this dying business around or to help Charlie make his MBO?"

He paused reflectively for a minute and said, "I dunno. Let me get back to you."

Two weeks later, he called. "Let's help Charlie make his MBO. Don't change the formula, but go ahead with the rest of the program, O.K.?"

O.K. it wasn't. What it was, was nuts! I'd fallen down the White Rabbit's hole. My only question now was, "Which one is he—the Mad Hatter or the March Hare?"

A few months later, we did it again.

"The Way We Do Things Around Here"

Jack Shipman, a young researcher in the Post Division, had applied some newfangled thing called "Psychographic Segmentation" to dog owners to produce what became a landmark study. It differentiated dog owners according to the reason they owned a dog in the first place—its purpose in the family. This explained the breed they chose and the way they cared for it. For example, one predominantly male group was "Hunters". Their dogs didn't actually have to hunt. They supported the owner's self-image as a hunter just because they were hunting breeds. Most stayed outside in a kennel because of the macho myth that "makin' 'em a housepet spoils 'em". (Actually, making a hunting dog a housepet strengthens the bond between dog and human. It makes whatever they do together, including hunting, work a lot better. But that's another subject.)

Hunter's dogs ate dry dog food almost exclusively. Occasionally, they got a few table scraps. They rarely got canned dog food. These dogs never saw a "treat" or anything a toy poodle might get. They wore plain brown leather collars. Their leashes were ropes or plain leather straps.

The group Jack identified that got my attention were the "Anthropomorphists". These were predominantly widows who lived alone or with another widow. They owned their dogs specifically to simulate human companionship. That's why Jack named them "Anthropomorphists." Their dogs were mostly lap dogs. They saw little dog food. They saw a lot of people food. They often had jeweled collars and leads and wore dog blankets and even booties. They not only slept indoors, they slept wherever they liked.

My other brand was Gaines™ Biscuits and Bits. These were multicolored, multiflavored dog treats that had a small share of market and a flat sales line. They were called dog biscuits because they were baked in an oven. Dogs liked their taste. The company believed these products competed in a mass market with all other dog biscuits.

Jack's study showed that plain MilkBone™ Dog Biscuits, by far the dominant product in the category, fit the "Family Dog" role exceptionally well. It had a dominant share of the market not because it broadly appealed to all dog owners but because it appealed strongly to a very large group of dog owners.

The Anthropomorphists never bought plain MilkBone™ biscuits, precisely because they *were* the archetypal dog biscuit. They bought cute treats like Liv-a-Snaps™, MilkBone™-flavored dog biscuits, cookies, crackers, and snacks. They were the primary buyers of Gaines™ Biscuits and Bits. These products helped this customer treat her dog more like a human. My product competed with cookies, crackers, snacks, and the most winsome of dog treats, not with plain MilkBone™ dog biscuits.

Think of the product's customers. Now, consider its package. A sterile white background with Gaines™ Biscuits stenciled across the front. Designed by the U.S. Army Corps of Engineers, perhaps? To warm it up, the designer added larger-than-life-size color illustrations of the biscuits. Ooooh! Those biscuits are so warm and cuddly!

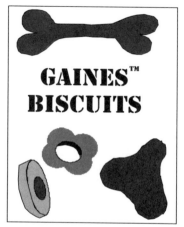

GAINES™
BISCUITS

I asked the art department to find photos of the breeds Anthropomorphists owned. "I want them to stare invitingly off the box, with pink tongue showing, just like the 'doggy in the window'. Get the brand name out of the way of the visual connection between the shopper and the dog," I told the artists. They did a great job. These packages oozed, "Let me sit on your lap."

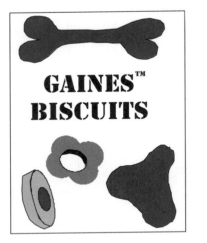 

Now tell me: If you're a little old lady with a lap dog, which of these packages speaks to you?

The total cost to change the package was $10,000 for new artwork and plates. When I recommended it, the marketing director said, "We can't. That package is changed every five years. This one is only three years old." I described what we'd learned about the customer. "People aren't really like that," he insisted. "That's sick—to replace a human with a dog. I don't believe it."

Aw, geeez, not again—and so soon.

About three years later, in a new job with a new company (surprise, surprise) I saw that "my" package had received the Pet Food Institute's Package of the Year award. I called the current brand manager. "Never mind the award. What effect did the package have on sales?" I asked. "I'm not exactly sure," he told me. "Since our package hit the market, Flavor Snacks has had some out-of-stocks. Some of the increase could be temporary. The closest I can estimate it is that sales have tripled. But they may have quadrupled."

Management by Frontal Lobotomy

When I left General Foods, I went to Puppy Palace. A start-up business, Puppy Palace was a chain of retail stores that sold purebred puppies and every dog-care product imaginable. M&M/Mars bought Puppy Palace as a side dish when it acquired Kal-Kan dog food.

The business started out to be a franchiseable concept. Unfortunately, it had none of the highly refined processes that make a franchise work. The founder had a span of control of about three stores. Once he had more than three, the business began unraveling like a cheap sweater. M&M/Mars replaced him. Their top troubleshooter became president. He brought some people with him. Norb Lauer, the vice-president of finance, was one. He developed not only the financial and MIS systems but also the extremely complex purchasing program necessary to keep at least twenty-two different breeds of puppies available in any one store at any time. He also developed a shared-compensation plan that motivated store personnel to put failing locations into the black. He was "Mr. Inside". I was "Mr. Outside". My title was vice-president of operations, which meant marketing, sales, and store operations.

Part of my job was to get people into the store. That was easy. It was full of puppies. Dealing with them once they got there was a lot harder.

We had to work from the true purpose of the business. From the Gaines study of dog owners, I knew that our real job was to provide the breed of dog that best suited the owner's reason for having a dog in the first place. Further, we had to provide puppy buyers with the same quality of purebred puppies they could get at a kennel, have a much wider selection of breeds to choose from, and have locations far more convenient than most kennels. The stores were in shopping malls. This provided easy access, but it disparaged the quality of the puppies. A store in a mall, filled with puppies, is a "pet shop". People perceive pet shop puppies to be of lower quality than those from kennels. We had to combat that perception, so we did everything we could to differentiate ourselves from pet shops. We gave health guarantees and full pedigrees. We carried only purebred puppies and dog supplies—no mutts, no cats, no fish, no birds, no anything that said "Pet Shop".

The trickiest job was converting store traffic into sales. Traffic was often heavy, but only 5 percent of U.S. households buy a puppy each year. We were competing for a share of that 5 percent. Only one of every twenty people that came through the door was a potential buyer. Finding them was the first trick. Completing the transaction was even harder. Purchasing a puppy is more like adopting a child than buying a product. Our job was to match the breed with the family's circumstances. We had to understand the role the dog was to play in the family and then pick the most appropriate breeds. Then, we had to let the chemistry happen between the people and the puppies. This took time and required well-developed counselor selling skills.

We developed the sales training and figured out how to find store people who had the talent to use it. In the next two years, we put all the internal and external systems into place. They worked. Store operations turned 180 degrees, from losing $3 million per year to making $3 million per year.

Two months after we realized we could make the business work, my boss called me in to discuss our store people. "Down deep, these guys are crooks," he said. "You have to install systems to catch them." Yes, a couple were dipping into the till. But most were not only honest; they also were dedicated to making their store successful. They'd demonstrated it. We treated them as the essential elements of success they were and almost all responded in kind. To treat them as felons yet to be caught was to destroy what worked—and the company with it.

A couple of weeks later, we had another meeting. "Now that we've got this thing going, Mars wants to speed up its return on investment. We've got to increase sales. We're going to put fish in the stores."

"Over my dead body" was out of my mouth before I had time to think about it.

We'd just spent two years differentiating ourselves from pet shops, and he'd figured out how to screw it up in one move. He'd made two suicidal decisions in two weeks. Where had this guy been for the past two years? At the time, I didn't understand what was going on. I just thought he'd stepped out for a quick frontal lobotomy.

As you might imagine, he took me up on my "over my dead body" remark. After I was gone, fish went into the stores and things "tightened up". "Strangled" would be more accurate. Seen any Puppy Palaces lately?

The People Food That People Couldn't Eat
(Raising the craziness quotient)

I joined Pillsbury as one of its two senior corporate new business development people. The first project I inherited was "solid instant breakfast". It was a good-for-you toaster product. It had a name and a package. The ad agency and my predecessor had already begun squabbling about the campaign, so it looked fairly close to launch. Well, maybe not.

On my desk one morning appeared eight, three-inch-wide, three-ring binders—filled.

"What's this?" I asked.

"This is your first project."

"How long has it been around? It takes a while to generate this much crap."

"Over three years."

"What's taking so long?"

"Well, we can't seem to get the product quite right."

"Wadda ya mean 'quite right'?"

"That's hard to describe."

"O.K., let's go over to the lab and take a look at it."

"Before you read the background?"

"Yes, before I read the background. You want to screw around for another three years?"

When we got to the lab, I met my R&D guy. He showed me the product. It looked like a small meadow muffin with orange ooze drizzled over it.

"I hope it tastes better than it looks," I remarked. "Pop it in the toaster, and let's find out."

"Why do you care what it tastes like?" the R&D guy asked.

My brain froze. *What the…??? Oh, God, not again.* But I trudged forward. This had to be good.

"Well, it's like this. This is a food product. What it tastes like affects whether or not people will eat it. Whether or not they'll eat it affects whether or not they'll buy it. For us to sell it, they have to buy it. If they won't eat it, they won't buy it. Then, we can't sell it, O.K.?"

"What it tastes like has nothing to do with whether or not they will buy it and eat it," he confidently assured me.

This was getting better and better. Somehow, the brain of my marketing director at General Foods had been implanted into this R&D guy at Pillsbury.

"Really?" I asked. "Where did you get that idea?"

"We have a $200,000 research study that shows people will buy it and eat it because of its nutritional value. Taste is immaterial."

"O.K., we have $200,000 of bullshit research. Now pop it in the toaster."

It actually tasted *worse* than it looked. And that was the *lesser* problem. It had the texture of strapping tape, complete with strands of reinforcing filament. The filaments were made from milk protein. They provided most of the product's nutritional value. They performed just like the filament in strapping tape. A person could not bite off a piece of solid instant breakfast, nor chew it. The only way to eat this product would be to chop it up with an ax and swallow each piece whole. The R&D boys had surpassed *wouldn't* eat. They'd achieved *couldn't* eat. That's got to be a milestone in food-product development.

I also found out that Pillsbury's new business development group had gotten into an argument about the results of the first market study with the ad agency, BBD&O. Pillsbury conducted the first study. After much bickering, BBD&O re-ran the study—using the same questionnaire. It simply omitted the issues of taste and texture. Yet the results were being used to show they weren't important. We actually had *$400,000* of bullshit market research.

I told my boss that we could either try to make the product both edible and nutritious, which would require finding new technology, or I could just kill the thing and go look for something with higher odds of success. At this point, that would have been almost anything.

He opted for the former. What the hell. The company had already invested $1.6 million in nutritious strapping tape. I assembled a new R&D

team. Six months and $600,000 later, we had a product that was both edible and nutritious.

I demonstrated the product to the group that would actually commercialize it, the general manager, directors, and the marketing people in the Grocery Products Division. They liked its taste. They believed its nutritional claims. The general manager said, "Great, turn it over. We'll take it to market."

"Not yet," I told him. "The product tastes O.K., but that doesn't mean it's a viable business."

"Why not?" he wanted to know.

"Well, in the process of making it both edible and nutritious, we've doubled its cost. For us to have enough profit margin to seriously consider commercializing this thing, its retail price will have to be more than twice that of Pop-Tarts™. I don't know if enough people will buy a good-for-you Pop-Tart™, at over twice the price, to make this a viable business."

"Of course they will," chipped in the marketing director. "We'll get it on grocery store shelves, tell consumers to buy it, and they will."

Sure they will—you #@**&# moron.

I refused to turn the product over. In retaliation, one, two, sometimes three members of the marketing group would visit my office every couple of days to ask me for it. One of the brand managers showed up one day when I was wearing down. "O.K.," I said. "I'll turn it over if you can give me one good reason why you'd invest $10 million to commercialize a product before we know if it's a viable business."

"Well, you know our liquid instant breakfast business is slipping. We're losing shelf space. We need something to hold space at retail."

"Let me get this straight," I countered. "You'd invest $10 million to put a product *on* grocery shelves without knowing whether or not it will come *off*, just to maintain shelf space for maybe no more than three to six months?"

"Sure!" he said cheerfully.

"Get out of my office."

But I did have the last laugh. I turned it over without any further testing because that's what this bunch deserved. It didn't live past the first home test. When they tried to ship it, they found it had a shelf life of about three days.

[Catch-22][3]

My new business development department's charter was to find new business opportunities in grocery product categories where Pillsbury *did not—NOT—*already compete. The company's new products had been dropping like concrete balloons. Why? It launched products into the marketplace with no clue about what consumers wanted. We were introducing irrelevant products.

To correct this, my new business development team originated an approach I call *use systems research*. It allowed us to understand what consumers were doing, their goal, their processes for achieving it, their satisfactions and dissatisfactions with these processes, the products they were using, and the results they were getting. It enabled us to define what they needed to do *their job* more effectively. That showed us how to create new products that would help them. These would have much higher odds of being successful as businesses. Self-evident truth, right?

My department wasn't the only group developing new product concepts; so were two outside new business consultancies and the internal marketing department for established products. Those three used the old "brainstorming" approach. All ideas were tested by Pillsbury's "supertest" of business potential. It separated those that were potentially viable businesses from those that weren't. The other three groups produced these results:

Source	Total Concepts Developed	Viable Businesses	Percent of Viable Businesses
Consulting Agency No. 1	26	0	0
Consulting Agency No. 2	6	1	17%
Marketing Department	40	3	7.5%
Totals	72	4	5.5%

Five and one-half percent is very close to the national average of truly new products that become successful businesses. In other words, 95 percent *don't* make it.

My team, applying "use systems research", created twenty-two new product concepts. Twelve were viable businesses. That's 54 percent, a potential success rate *ten times higher* than the traditional approach.

I presented the results to management, told them why the results were so different, and recommended we adopt the new approach.

"But that's not the way it's done," they responded.

"Yes, I know," I said. "The way it's done gets you 5 percent success. That's my whole point."

"But that's just not the way it's done," they repeated.

The warden of their minds had sounded the alarm for a general lock down.

Whenever I'd follow my charter and present a new business opportunity in a product category where Pillsbury did not—*NOT*—already participate, management would reject it because, "We're not in that business." This is a perfect Catch-22. The reason to do something and to *not* do it is the same reason.

While these fiascoes were playing out, Pillsbury got a new CEO. I met him at a clubby little meeting, "The Marketing Roundtable". "How's it going?" he asked.

I told him. "Creating a new business around here is like running a marathon that's really an obstacle course. At the starting line, everybody is cheering. There's plenty of water—which you don't need. The gun goes off. As you go along, you notice that the crowd is thinning out and the water stations are getting fewer and farther between. Suddenly, you see guys erecting blockades up ahead. It finally dawns on you that if you're going to finish this race, you'll have to do it in spite of the company, not with its help."

"That's the best description of new business development around here I've ever heard," he rejoined.

Whoa! Had I found an ally? I pushed forward. "Well, what are you going to do about it?"

"Nothing," he said. "It's my opinion that if you'd work for us, you couldn't pull it off, anyway."

The CEO had just told one of the company's two senior business development people that he had his job because top management believed he couldn't do it. Combine that with, "We can't do it a better way because that's not the way it's done" and "We can't go into that business because we're not already in that business", and we have [Catch-22][3].

This isn't just garden-variety nonsense. This is the anti-sense that leads to the view that meaning does not and cannot exist. This was when the question, "How come my best stuff gets me into the most trouble?" showed up on my big screen, with full orchestral support. And what happened to these businesses and companies?

Gaines™ Meal died. So did Gaines™ Biscuits and Bits. General Foods was acquired by Philip Morris, which sold off Gaines and Birds-Eye and merged what was left with Kraft Foods. Puppy Palace died. Pillsbury was wholly acquired by Grand Metropolitan in a hostile takeover. About 50 percent of its employees were fired. Then the company was taken private. Score: One company dismembered. One company dead and buried. One company bedridden.

Did anybody win? I lost. So did many other employees. So did the customers. Top management won, temporarily, then lost. Let's see, that's lose—lose—lose—win—oops, no, lose. This is the disease of aging systems. Clinical symptoms: long periods of walking death, sometimes coma, and, eventually, the material death of the organization or institution. This disease infects people. People contract nonsense when they are immersed in it. They aren't born nonsensical.

In the next several chapters, we'll find the root cause of the insanity I've just described. In the process, we'll discover how to find meaning and why that's been so difficult. The ability to make these discoveries lies in understanding complex systems.

The real voyage of discovery consists not in seeking new landscapes, but in having new eyes.

— Marcel Proust

Chapter Two
The Basics of Systems

This is the context we must have to be able to see the *essential* reason why meaning has been so difficult to find. Defining a problem at its root cause makes its solution obvious—not easy, just obvious.

When I was a kid, what annoyed me most about adults was their attitude that everything worth knowing was already known. If they were right, everything should be working just great. A quick glance around dispelled that notion. The odds were pretty good that everything worth knowing *wasn't* already known.

Complex systems are worth knowing. Until recently, we haven't even acknowledged systems, let alone understood them. Life—reality—is a complex system composed of complex systems. If we're not even aware of the basic nature of systems, how competent *can we be* at life? Our education, training, and experience rarely contain a systems view of any subject. Yet everything we know and have ever known, from atoms to our universe, from an individual embryo to ecosystems composed of thousands of interdependent life forms, is a complex system. Being unaware of systems amounts to having no idea what life is about.

We can study things—animals, plants, machines, social institutions—in isolation, and generate information about them. But to know what the information *means*, we have to *see* it in the context of the system it came from. And every system participates in a larger system. A deer is a complex system that is part of a larger, more complex ecosystem. A machine is a complex system that is part of a larger, more complex system of production. People must be able to *see* systems in order to find meaning. That's the first clue to why meaning is so hard to find. We have no frame of reference for it. So let's rectify that glaring omission. First, the basics:

1. What is a system? Let's make sure we're at least talking about the same thing.

2. The structure of systems. Until a person knows how a system is structured, he or she has no context for understanding the relationship between its component parts, or which is cause and which is effect.

3. The states of systems. Systems have two major states—intangible and tangible.

   All systems have an originating cause, an original purpose. That purpose actualizes itself in a particular environment. The combination of original intent and environment defines the system's design. This is its intangible state. That design then materializes as forms and processes for accomplishing its purpose in its particular environment. The forms and processes are its tangible state. To find meaning, we have to find the purpose behind the material forms.

4. The hierarchy of systems. Systems are interconnected—hierarchically. Any one system is a component of a larger system. We have to understand the larger system in order to understand its component subsystems.

5. The types of systems. There are two — open and closed. The difference between them is the difference between being alive and being a machine.

What Is a System?

Webster's dictionary tells us that a system is "a regularly interacting or interdependent group of items forming a unified whole". That's only part of the story. Their "items"—component parts—are diverse and dissimilar, yet they combine to achieve a single purpose. They are diverse both in function (what they do) and in form (how they do it). Yet the system is a unified, integrated entity. "Integrated diversity" is an uncommon conception in Western thinking, so here's an example. It's far simpler than human systems because it's inanimate—a bathroom sink.

A bathroom sink is a relatively simple complex system. It's composed of two shutoff valves, one connected to a cold-water supply, the other to a hot-water supply. They are operated by handles. They're connected to a faucet and mounted on a bowl that has a drain and a drain stop. Pipes deliver water to the sink. A water pump moves it from a well to a pressure tank. Some goes to a hot-water heater, then to the sink. Cold water moves directly from the pressure tank to the sink. This is "interaction forming a unified whole".

The sink's components are diverse in both function and form. The shutoff valves prevent the flow of water. They are metal or a composite. They screw open and closed. The bowl holds water. It's ceramic. It has no moving parts. The pipes transport water. They are either copper or PVC. The pump provides the force that actually moves the water. It's electromechanical and has moving parts. If you simply laid the components of this system side by side, you'd be hard pressed to find similarity among them. They perform different functions, use different processes, come in different shapes and sizes and are made from different materials. This is a highly diverse system of components. That diversity is absolutely necessary for the sink to accomplish its purpose.

The unifying factor is the sink's purpose—to facilitate a person's ability to wash his or her hands and face.

Systems cannot be effective without diversity. They must have it to have the range of capabilities necessary to accomplish their purpose. That's why systems that attempt to minimize diversity become ineffective, weak, impotent, and, eventually, die.

Diversity among a system's components often confuses us. When we focus only on differences, we can't see the purpose that creates the unified whole. We fail to ask *why* something is the way it is. Yet *Why?* is the question that reveals meaning.

The Structure of Systems

The world abounds in graphic representations of systems. They exist in all cultures and date back to the earliest days of prehistory. All people, from pre-Celtic stonemasons to modern theoretical physicists, have depicted them in similar ways. They are concentric circles, ellipses, and spirals with an undercurrent of motion. We see this pattern in our solar system and in our image of atoms.

Eastern and Native American theologies use symbols of systems as images of their philosophies.

Fractals are mathematically calculated images of systems.

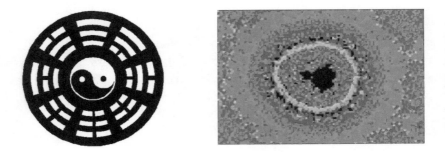

Notice that they all resemble throwing a stone into a pond—ripples emanating from a central, originating event. That event is the system's originating cause, its purpose. Call it root, essence, seed, core, nucleus, originating force, or organizing principle. Whatever you call it, it defines the system—what it is, what it will produce, how it will produce it, what its component parts will be, how they will be organized, and the nature of their relationship. A single egg cell, just after it has been impregnated by a sperm cell, is a good example. This unity has the complete set of genetically encoded instructions for creating the entire physical system—

the new member of its species. The offspring is the physical manifestation of this originating design.

We spend our lives in the ripples—the forms and processes—the tangible, physical states of systems—ignorant of their originating event. That's why we don't know what things mean. For life's tangibles to have meaning, we have to discover their originating cause. *Recognizing that a system emanates from a central, originating, and unifying force is the single most critical aspect of understanding systems—and finding meaning.*

A system's core is its purpose, the primary cause of all its effects—forms, processes, and results produced. Purpose defines what it must recruit from its environment in order to manifest itself. Let's say the intent is to move people and goods from place to place, over land. In an industrial environment that has the internal combustion engine, that intent manifests itself as cars and trucks. In an earlier agricultural environment, that intent manifested itself as wagons, buggies, and carts drawn by oxen and horses. These are totally different forms that have the same intent, exhibited in different environments.

Intent gives the system, and all its component parts, their meaning. It's the yardstick by which everything in the system does or does not make sense. It makes no sense to build vehicles to move people from place to place, over land, that don't enable them to sit down because people get tired and cranky when they stand for long periods.

Human social institutions are no different. They begin as an intent, a purpose, something someone wants to accomplish. The original intent of governments, educational systems, religions, businesses, entire societies was to increase human well-being. Remember this, because the disease of social institutions that makes things meaningless comes from disregarding this original intent.

The States of Systems

The metaphor of a stone thrown into a pond works not only because it describes the structure of a system and places the appropriate emphasis on its origin but also because it accurately represents the original nature of any system. When a stone hits water, it transfers energy to the water, which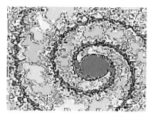

emanates from the source as waves—ripples. This is also true of systems, particularly human social systems. They begin as energy. They materialize "out of nothing". Their origins are either so small that they are invisible or are literally immaterial, that is, not material—a concept, an idea. An "Aha!" is pure psychic energy. A successful idea is psychic energy given material form. Therefore, systems have two very different *states*— an invisible, intangible, original state of cause and a tangible, subsequent state of effect. They're as different as

Our Mind's Eye

H_2O in its gaseous state (water vapor) and H_2O in its solid state (ice) *only because of form*. They have exactly the same *content*. H_2O is always H_2O, whether it's steam, water, or ice. Meaning is found in the system's essential nature, its content. It's easiest to see in the original, intangible state. We can't find it through our physical senses. We can't hear it, touch it, taste it, smell it, or even see it with our eyes. We can only see it in our mind's eye. If our mind's eye isn't in good working order, we're blind to meaning.

I had a hard time deciding what to call the intangible state of a system. Western society is so oriented to material forms that English offers little to choose from where the intangible is concerned. We have "spiritual", "metaphysical", "function", and "soul". "Spiritual" is probably the most commonly used when we mean "not material", but it's loaded with supernatural, mystical, and religious connotations that say "not for human comprehension". The last thing I wanted to do was give it these connotations. "Metaphysical" and "soul" have the same problem. "Function" doesn't, but it's often used to mean process rather than the *intent* of the process—how something works rather than the reason it exists.

Thanks to Archie Bahm, a professor of philosophy at the University of New Mexico, I found an obscure word in his translation of *Tao Teh King* (also known as *Tao Te Ching*) that means precisely what I intend by the intangible state of systems: *Mana*. Anthropologists use this word to denote the intangible causes of tangible effects. Bahm defines it as "prior in nature to any distinction between personal and impersonal, rational and irrational, one and many, spirit and matter." This was exactly what I wanted. It's the original simple unity, preceding the system's complex of components, which determines what they must be, what they do, their relationship to each other.

An idea is *Mana*. So are "Aha!," "Eureka!" epiphanies, and "Getting it"—blinding glimpses of the obvious when all the pieces come together to disclose the whole. I decided against using *Mana*, however, because its dictionary definition is "a dynamic supernatural power", and because it also conjures up "manna from heaven". Either way, I was back where I didn't want to be. I finally decided to use "spirit" because we *occasionally* use it to mean "the original intent", as in "the spirit of the law" or "the spirit of the moment". I use it here to mean *only* the intangible state of systems that contain original intent—ideas, mind's eye images, the "Aha!"s of life—creative thinking and perception. It has no moralistic or theological qualities. It *is* metaphysical only because it *precedes* the material or physical. It *is* transcendental because it transcends separate parts to recognize their unity. *Used this way, "spirit" is entirely within the realm of natural human capacity.*

Looking to symbolize the spiritual state of a system, I first considered the Tao. It symbolizes the reconciliation of opposites as complementary halves of the whole. In the *Tao Teh King*, which Archie Bahm interpreted as "Nature and Intelligence", Lao Tzu wrote:

> In fact, all distinctions naturally appear as opposites. And opposites get their meaning from each other and find their completion only through each other. The meaning of "is" and "is not" arise from our distinguishing between them.

But I wanted a symbol that more accurately represented the dynamics of a system's origin. All system origins have an intent that unifies its two principal complements. They're definitely different from each other. We might view them as opposites but not antagonists. A man and a woman create a child. Sodium and chlorine create salt. Water and flour make a cake. Plants and animals are complements of ecosystems, exchanging oxygen, carbon dioxide, and nutrients that enable each other's survival. Companies and customers exchange products or services for money.

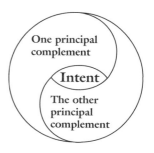

One principal complement

Intent

The other principal complement

Simply overlapping the two complements, designating the overlap as the area of common purpose—the intent—and changing the symbol to shades of gray to eliminate the connoted antagonism of black and white, accurately represents these originating dynamics.

Knowing the system's originating purpose allows us to "see" what it, and everything in it, *means*. Purpose—intent—is the *source* of meaning, which we can only see in our "mind's eye".

Once the originating intent is defined, the system moves toward its material state. We see this in everything we create—buildings, machines, new products and services, and social institutions—government, education,

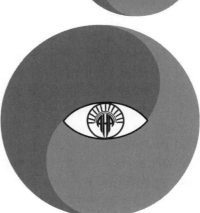

religious philosophies. The first step is to identify, considering the environment in which the system will exist, possible forms and processes for accomplishing its purpose. This is the system's design. It is still intangible. The work required is creative thinking and problem-solving. Its most tangible output is a description, in words and/or pictures, of the intended result and the means of achieving it—the plan, the blueprint. This completes the system's spiritual state. Throughout this book I'll be using these symbols to represent the spiritual state of systems.

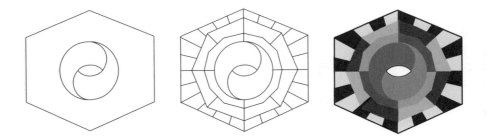

As systems develop, they generate the processes and physical components required to achieve their purpose. At each successive level of development, components become more concrete, more specific. Each accounts for a smaller portion of the total system than its predecessor. In other words, the system becomes more complex. Its components become more specialized. Think of a piece of music played by its composer on a piano. Now think about it played by an orchestra. The original system for moving people from place to place over land was on foot—very simple. Then came the horse and buggy—more complex but still relatively simple. Next came the automobile, with all its interconnected, moving parts. Now, think of cars forty or fifty years ago, when their owners could still work on them. Then, think of them today. That's the progression—simple beginnings to ever-increasing complexity *for achieving the same purpose*. Sometimes increased complexity more effectively achieves the original purpose. In human systems it often doesn't, because it *obscures* the original purpose.

The graphic at right represents the development of the whole system. It progresses from few, larger, more circular, gray (inclusive) spaces at the center to many, smaller, straight-lined, black-and-white (exclusive) spaces on the perimeter. It originates as comprehensive, intangible *function* that develops into concrete, complex *form*. It can also be described as originating as intangible *cause* of tangible *effects*.

Perhaps the most fundamental way to distinguish between the spiritual and material states of systems is to think of the physical world. The material state of a system can be seen or smelled or tasted or heard or felt; sometimes all five senses come into play. A system's material state exists in the dimensions of space and time. A system's spiritual state doesn't. It exists only in someone's mind's eye. It occupies no space. The whole system can be seen at once, so it is also independent of time. Energy is spiritual state. Matter is material state. Spiritual state is cause. Material state is effect.

These two states, combined, accomplish the system's original purpose. I added a border to the graphic on the following page to illustrate this outcome. *The outcome is the material form of the originating*

The outcome is the material form of the originating intent.

intent. I once heard Watts Wacker, a business futurist and lecturer, say, "A product is an artifact of a promise." The *promise* is spiritual. The *product* is its manifestation, its material state. The spiritual state of a system is simple. Its material state is complex. The older and more developed it is, the more complex its form. Understanding what all that complexity *means* requires understanding the system in its original spiritual state.

The Relationship of Systems to Each Other

Understanding how one system relates to another is about more than simple interconnectedness. It's about where meaning comes from—*why* any given system has the purpose it does.

Every system is also a component of a larger system. The larger system in which it participates determines its nature. To illustrate this, I'll use an abbreviated graphic for systems. It has three major elements:

Purpose   Component parts   The organization and relationship of component parts.

Putting them together gives us this symbol.

To see how systems relate to each other, let's go back to the bathroom sink. It's a system in its own right. Nearby are a tub, shower, toilet, towels on racks, cleansers, shaving instruments, and so on. Each of these is also a system. Along with the sink, they comprise a larger, more complex system—a bathroom. A bathroom sink is a system for removing dirt and wastes from hands and face. A tub or shower is a system for removing dirt and wastes from the rest of the outer body. A toilet is a system for removing inner-body wastes. In total, a bathroom is a system for removing dirt and wastes from the human body. That's *why* we have what we have in bathrooms.

Next to the bathroom are two bedrooms, then a study, then a living room, a kitchen, and a mud room—additional complex systems that constitute a still larger, more complex system, a house. In total, its purpose is to support physical, mental, and emotional human vitality. Each room, which is one of its subsystems, supports a specific part of that purpose.

Houses comprise communities. Communities comprise the residential portion of societies—and so on and so on.

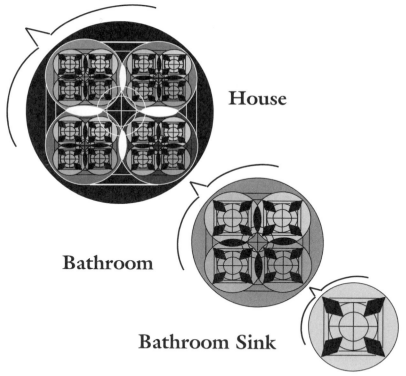

House

Bathroom

Bathroom Sink

This is the relationship of systems. It's a hierarchy. Every system interacts with others as components of a larger, more complex system. At each level, the purpose of the larger system determines the purpose of the systems within it. Why? *Because a system's components exist only to enable it to accomplish its purpose.*

Everything we know, everything that is—atom, universe, box of dirt, dog, house, company, nation—is a system. Our universe is organized and structured on *purpose*. We can't be certain of the purpose behind those systems humans didn't originate, although we've created a lot of mythology and religion to try to comprehend them. We *can* identify the purpose of systems we *did* originate.

We do or do not find meaning in our lives within the context of our social systems. Are they structured like other systems? Absolutely. Consider the institution of "business." An individual business is part of a company. The company is part of an industry. Industries comprise the business sector of society, which includes many sectors or subsystems: education, government and law, arts, religion, science, and business.

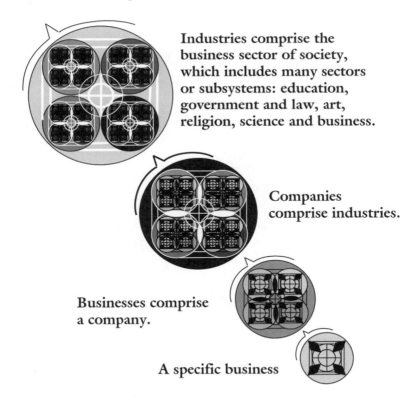

Industries comprise the business sector of society, which includes many sectors or subsystems: education, government and law, art, religion, science and business.

Companies comprise industries.

Businesses comprise a company.

A specific business

Let's keep going. Societies are subsystems of the human race. Humans, along with other animals, plants, insects, water, land, and air, form ecosystems. Ecosystems make up the major system, Earth. This is why ecologists are legitimately concerned. The animal most capable of altering systems is virtually unaware of them.

Obviously, if you push this progression far enough, Earth to our solar system, solar systems to galaxies, galaxies to universe, you end up at the whole of it all, which many people call "God". That's fine. But our current proficiency suggests that the human race requires centuries of intensive skill development in systems before we try to define God. As you'll see, we've defined God in man's image, contrary to the popular notion that God made man in His image. The latter may turn out to be true, but at this point in human evolution, we're in no position to know. We have to start somewhere. Finding meaning in our own lives is as good a place as any.

Open and Closed Systems

Systems that acknowledge their interdependence with their environment are *open* systems. Systems that don't are *closed*. This is the difference between being alive and being a machine.

Machines are closed systems. They can only do what they were built to do, the way they were built to do it. When some change in their environment occurs, they have no innate ability to adjust to it. They lose their relevance. When this happens, machines become obsolete.

A chemical reaction that has reached stable equilibrium is a naturally occurring example of a closed system. Its principal elements are no longer exchanging electrons and absorbing or releasing energy in the process. The system is inert. Energy has been perfectly, evenly distributed. It has reached maximum entropy—*the lack of energy available to do work*. Had it once been alive, it would now be dead.

Living things are open systems. They adjust what they do and how they do it in relation to the conditions they face, minute by minute, day by day, to optimize their chances of survival and well-being. We call them "adaptive" because they work to sustain their relevance, their connection with their environment. This continual interaction causes tension and demands changed responses. Many people, especially traditional psychologists, view *absence* of tension as the desired state of being. That's the human equivalent of the chemical reaction that reached stable equilibrium or, in biological terms, "homeostasis". It's a state of *maximum* entropy—inert, dead, or, in mental and emotional terms, bored. The tension caused by interaction with the environment *prevents entropy*. It *renews life*. The challenge of creating new responses drives the system back to its core purpose. It reinvents its forms and processes. It reinvents itself. That's how it re-energizes.

Humans—individual people and social systems—can choose to be either open or closed. In an open social system, each principal complement recognizes the other and the intent that unifies them. In a closed social system, each recognizes only itself—not the other, not the unifying intent. This is the essential difference between actually being alive and pursuing a mechanical imitation of life.

An Open Social System   A Closed Social System

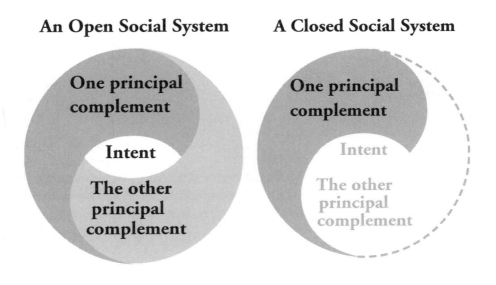

In closed systems—institutions—the people in charge of maintaining the status quo force the rest to operate like robots. This produces entropy. Through it, these systems bring about their own demise.

In open systems, people get *intrinsic* satisfaction from continually interacting with the other principal complement of the system. They use their individual creativity to solve present problems under present conditions. This perpetuates the system's well-being.

Here's a summary of the critical differences between *open* and *closed* systems.

	Open System	Closed System
Primary Driving Force	The system's originating purpose, the result it intends to produce.	Disregards original purpose. Concerns itself with refining its forms and processes.
Relationship with Environment	Connected, integrated with environment.	Disconnected, isolated from environment.
Nature of Steady State or State of Balance	Dynamic—constantly reinvents forms or processes to sustain its purpose. This replenishes the system's energy and minimizes entropy.	Static—constantly strives for control and "rigidification" of processes. This prevents replenishing energy and maximizes entropy.
Perspective	Integrative, synthesizing. Sees wholes, their interdependent parts, and understands the relationship between them.	Linear and dissective— Analytical. Sees parts in isolation, disconnected from one another.

Open and Closed System Origins

Only things that have an inherent life force can create and develop new systems. Systems are of no concern to machines or rocks (as far as I know). Systems may originate as either closed or open. The difference lies in whether the system's originating purpose recognizes and unifies both its principal complements or whether the defined intent benefits only the system's creator. The former is an *open* approach. The latter is *closed*. For example, if a company defines the intent of a new product without knowing what would be beneficial to potential users of that product, that's a closed approach. If a company deliberately develops a product or service to provide what it knows will be distinctly beneficial to users, that's an open approach.

Traditional evolution theory is a closed-system view of the creation of new species—new systems. This theory contends that new systems are not deliberately created to be more relevant, better adapted to their environment. Those that prosper adapt very effectively, but this ability comes from accidents of gene recombination rather than from purposeful, knowledgeable design. This is "survival of the [randomly occurring] fittest", which, by the way, doesn't mean the biggest, strongest, meanest son of a bitch in the valley. It means those most capable of integrating or fitting into their environment.

Richard Dawkins, a British biologist and author of *The Selfish Gene*, recognized the limitations of the random recombination approach and described an alternative that is closer to an open, purposeful system:

> Survival machines that can simulate the future are one jump ahead of survival machines who can only learn on the basis of trial and error. The trouble with overt trial is that it takes time and energy. The trouble with overt error is that it is often fatal. Simulation is both safer and faster.

Simulation means testing the design of several new systems to find the one that best integrates the creator of the system with its environment. Trial and error means randomly developing new systems and tossing them into their environment. Only a tiny percent of these survive.

To show the difference between originating a system as *closed* or *open*, let's say our intent is: "To drain the swamp". I'm using this old metaphor to put a little fun into illustrating the point, so please overlook its ecological ignorance. The organization that will develop the drainage device is one principal complement. The swamp is the other.

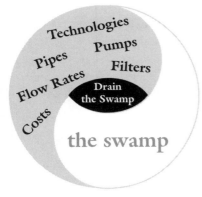

In the closed-system approach, engineers would first collect information about swamp-draining technology. They'd study pumps, pipes, flow rates, and filters. Based on this, they'd design a drainage mechanism. Think of this as a problem-solution situation. The creators of the solution have no specific knowledge of the problem. That's why it's a closed approach. It ignores the other principal complement, the specific system in which the solution will be applied: the swamp.

With blueprint in hand, contractors install the equipment in a specific swamp. This is when everybody realizes there might have been a better way to do it.

Taking an open approach, the engineers first acknowledge the other principal complement—*which* swamp to drain. How large is it? How much water does it hold? How firm is the bottom? What kind of vegetation does it contain? What is the capacity of the catch basin into which the water will drain? What flow rate prevents that basin from overflowing? What's the alligator population?

After they understand the nature of the problem, the engineers figure out how to solve it. They create a drainage mechanism most appropriate to that particular swamp.

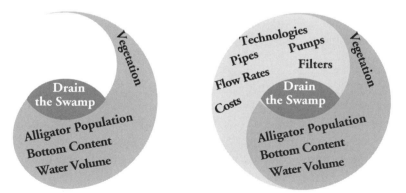

The difference between the two approaches shows up in the results they produce.

The Closed-System Approach

Most Likely Results

Implementation

Technologies
Pipes Pumps
Filters
Flow Rates
Drain
Costs the Swamp

Install Drainage System in Swamp

Up to Your Ass in Alligators

The Open-System Approach

Most Likely Results

Implementation

Technologies
Pipes Pumps
Filters
Flow Rates
Drain
Costs the Swamp
Alligator population
Bottom Content
Water Volume

Install Drainage System in Swamp

A Drained Swamp

Not just at birth but at any stage of its lifecycle, a closed system is much more likely to find itself up to its ass in alligators than an open system.

Summary

Complex systems are diverse components organized to achieve a single purpose. Purpose determines what a system will be, what component parts it will have, and how those components will function together to achieve the system's intent.

Systems have two basic states—their spiritual state and their material state. Neither is complete without the other. A system's origin, its spiritual state, is intangible. It is visible only to the mind's eye. *Its spiritual state is also the only place its meaning can be seen*. A system's material state is the physical manifestation of its intent. *The material state, by itself, is meaningless*.

The origin of all systems is the integration of two principal complements through a unifying intent or purpose. Neither principal complement is complete without the other. The spiritual state shows this core purpose and the two principal complements it unites. Remember the bathroom sink? Its intent is to facilitate the washing of hands and face. The two principal complements are the maker of the sink and those who use it. Its spiritual state is a picture in the mind of a design engineer. Its material state is that complex of valves, pipes, and bowl that manifest the design.

Every system—a complex system in its own right—is also a component of a larger complex system. Its purpose and nature are determined by the system in which it participates.

In an open system, each principal complement is open to, that is, cognizant of and tightly connected to the other. Recognition of interdependence unites them. Open, *adaptive* systems continuously modify their forms and processes to sustain this connection in the face of changing conditions.

When systems originate as closed systems, they are not deliberately designed to integrate effectively with their environmental partner(s). Some do, but only by chance. They survive. Most don't. They die shortly after birth.

Life, reality, is a complex of complex systems. Each is founded on a purpose. Purpose is the basis of meaning. Why, then, do we have so much trouble finding meaning in our lives? Because our social institutions are closed systems. They train us, as people, to be closed systems. How they do that is the subject of the next chapter.

Then came the churches, then came the schools,
then came the lawyers, then came the rules…

—Mark Knopfler, "Telegraph Road"

Chapter Three
The Lifecycle of Social Systems

We participate in social systems—family life, friendships, work life, religious life. We either get a sense of meaning from this participation or we don't. The nature of the system, our role in it, and our view of that role determine whether or not it means anything to us. Since our purpose here is to find meaning in our lives, we need to understand the nature of human social institutions.

George Land is a general systems practitioner. He wrote *Grow or Die* and, with Beth Jarman, *Breakpoint and Beyond*. I worked with him on a 3M program called "Living Innovation". He applied general systems theory to social institutions. He showed that institutions go through at least two major phases—formative and normative. Most die at the end of their normative phase. However, a third phase, rebirth, is possible. He called this the integrative phase. What's important to us is the nature of these phases because of the impact they have on people.

In the very beginning, a social institution is completely intangible. It originates as a purpose, a concept, an idea, a philosophy, a solution to a problem in someone's mind. People then move to manifest it—give it a form that will undertake the processes that accomplish its purpose. That gives it a material state. We call the material state "reality", even though it's only the material portion of reality, because our physical senses—sight, hearing, touch, taste, smell—can detect it. The system moves from the intangible to the tangible, from the spiritual to the material, from concern with function (the *why*) to concern with form and process (the *how*). In physical terms, we could say it begins as an invisible gas, then a flexible solid, then a rigid mobile solid, and finally a rigid immobile solid. It moves from pure energy to petrified matter. Finally, it shatters and dies—unless it recreates itself by recognizing its original, spiritual state.

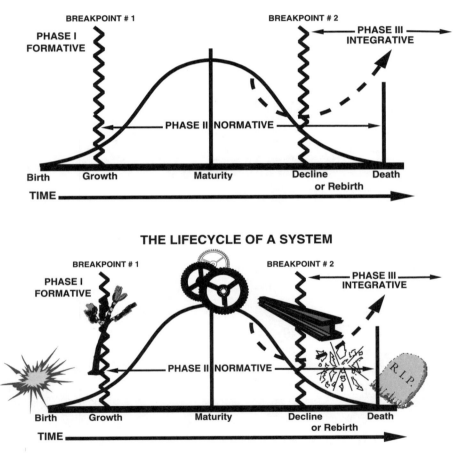

THE LIFECYCLE OF A SYSTEM

THE LIFECYCLE OF A SYSTEM

The Formative Phase

When people are creating a system, that system is in its formative phase. They begin with a purpose. Then, they design the means for accomplishing that purpose. Through several stages, they develop the practices, processes, and tangible forms that actualize their intent. The system journeys from spiritual to material. For example, a new religious philosophy recruits adherents, develops symbols and artifacts, and builds places of worship. These comprise the physical form of the founding philosophy.

Originating Purpose

The formative phase may be either open or closed. If open, it recognizes both of the system's principal complements, so that its purpose is beneficial to both. If closed, the creators consider only their own benefit.

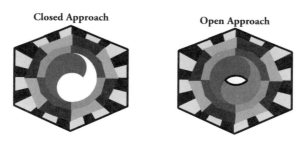

Whether open or closed, the formative phase requires making it up as you go along. It involves constant creative problem-solving. Forming a new business, for example, requires not only creating the product or service; it also demands creating all the abilities to get it into the marketplace.

Once a system prospers, by accident or design, it moves into its normative phase. This is usually the beginning of its end.

The Normative Phase

The normative phase of *all* systems have the same purpose, which is completely independent from the originating purpose of any specific system. The goal of the formative phase was to figure out how to materialize the system's intent. The goal of the normative phase is to maximize the *efficiency* of the forms and processes it created to do that, whatever they were. That's why the transition is called a "breakpoint"—new goal, new rules. The formative way of working no longer applies.

To focus on maximizing efficiency, regardless of the specific nature of the system, the people in charge during the normative phase accept, uncritically, whatever *content* already exists. *What* "we do around here" is a given. Their concern is confined to doing it more efficiently and effectively. They epitomize the attitude that everything substantive that's worth knowing is already known. After all, it works, doesn't it? Their job is to maximize predictability. This means eliminating diversity and variance. Maximizing predictability includes ensuring that everyone in the system also accepts, unquestioningly, whatever already exists. The question is always, "<u>Are we doing things right?</u>" It is never, "Are we doing the right things?" <u>The normative phase is about control and conformity</u>. This is "management".

The premise of *Breakpoint and Beyond* is that mankind is approaching the second major breakpoint in its history, the transformation from normative to integrative systems. But what was its first breakpoint, the rise of normative systems? According to Land and Jarman, it was the rise of civilization itself. That makes sense. The major difference between pre- and post-civilization life was man's mode of survival. Before "civilization", man was nomadic. People didn't know what tomorrow would bring. Hell, they didn't know what was behind the next rock. Evidently some genius decided that the not-knowing (lack of predictability) was the primary reason life was so difficult and attributed it to the constant wandering. The answer: stop moving, stop facing new situations every day, every week.

Civilization meant staying in one place—settling. Rather than seeing many new things every day, people now saw many familiar things every day. They felt more secure.

A nomadic existence is, quite literally, making it up as you go along—a perpetually formative existence in which creativity is linked directly to survival. Civilization is the opposite. It's built for repetition—doing the same things, the same way, under the same conditions, day after day after day. That's "normative". Civilization overtly punishes creativity, because creativity produces variance and decreases predictability. That's O.K. up to the point of establishing a stable platform on which to work. But beyond that point, the drive for predictability becomes a prison of conformity that drives out the diversity needed for vitality. The civilization weakens and dies. These dynamics apply to every level of human existence—an individual person, one-to-one personal relationships, social organizations such as companies, social institutions such as business, education, and religion, entire societies, and even civilization itself.

Human existence went from one extreme to the other—from constant variation to constant repetition. Either one alone is insufficient. Constant variation prevents building and spreading a body of knowledge about what works and what doesn't. Constant repetition prevents the growth of knowledge and understanding that permits adaptation. It eventually causes the death of the system.

Viewed this way, the human race has more to fear from civilization than from atomic warfare. In fact, all forms of Armageddon are the *result* of closed, normative systems. All that changes is scale.

If you're a student of history, you've seen normative dynamics in the decline and fall of societies, some of the most notable being Greece, the Roman Empire, and, most recently, the USSR. If you're a student of business, you've seen normative dynamics in the decline and fall of individual businesses, companies and entire industries—the American steel and automotive industries, for example.

The Japanese were able to capture more than 30 percent of the American car market because of such dynamics. In his book *Iacocca*, Lee Iacocca recounts trying to convince Henry Ford III that Americans wanted more fuel-efficient cars. Mr. Ford's response in effect, was, "Americans want big powerful gas guzzlers, and that's what we're going to give them." This is the man in charge of a normative system doing his job—demanding adherence to the established rules in the face of powerful evidence they no longer apply. This is how normative systems commit suicide.

A normative system is entirely concerned with the mechanics of material existence—effects. That consumption excludes a view of spiritual existence— cause. Therefore, a normative viewpoint is blind to what things *mean*. That's why man's search for meaning is both so difficult and such an old, old subject. Civilization effectively outlawed meaning 8,000 years ago. Of course, there have been many people who have resisted the idea of life without meaning. We know how many of them ended up, don't we? And let that be a warning to the rest of us.

Normative systems are concerned exclusively with the material. They actively ignore the spiritual.

As any system grows, its functions become more developed. They specialize. But nature doesn't normalize. Living things—open, adaptive systems—go directly from their formative phase to an integrative phase. They refine their operating subsystems in accord with their primary purpose. Thus, the subsystems evolve interdependently. One does not develop in isolation from or in conflict with another because that would weaken the larger system's chances of survival. The claws of successive generations of

Living systems specialize interdependently, to more effectively achieve their original purpose

tigers may become sharper and stronger, permitting faster catches and kills. The heart of a mammal that depends on flight for survival might increase its pumping capacity so as to deliver more oxygen and energy to muscles, while removing toxins faster. In an ant colony, the workers might develop greater capability to gather food supplies during adverse weather while the soldiers develop greater ability to resist attacks.

In contrast, almost all human social institutions, whether open or closed in their formative phase, become closed soon after birth. Specialization takes a very different form. Subsystems and components specialize *independently*. People concentrate on refining and standardizing the forms and processes of their function, ignorant of the reason it exists in the first place—its meaning. People focus more and more on pieces rather than wholes. The "big picture" gets smaller and dimmer. This is bureaucracy. A bureaucrat is not only unconcerned with citizens or customers. He also doesn't know or care what other departments, or even the person seated next to him, are about. This fragmentation eventually disintegrates the system.

While thousands of living species have survived and evolved for hundreds of thousands of years, a few hundred years is the high end of life expectancy for human social institutions—except for religions, which we'll talk about later in this chapter.

Remember the old story of the little girl who asked her mother why she always cut the end off a ham before she baked it? Mother answered, "Because my mother did." The girl then asked her grandmother why she cut the end off the ham before she baked it. Her grandmother answered, "Because my mother did." Great-grandmother was still alive, so the little girl asked her why she did it. "Because my roasting pan was too small for the average-sized ham," replied Great-Grandma. That's normalizing—attention to form and process, oblivious to cause—the "why" behind the action. It's "monkey see, monkey do"—unexamined imitation. By definition, it's meaningless.

One of my friends has a favorite rhetorical question: "Have you had twenty-five years of experience or one year of experience twenty-five times?" A normative person in the normative phase of a system has "one year of experience twenty-five times". It's doing the same things, the same way, over and over and over again. Those who refuse this kind of existence are labeled "nonconformists". When Socrates said, "An unexamined life isn't worth living", he was referring to this condition. It isn't worth living because it's devoid of meaning. An "unexamined life"—mindless repetition of activities without understanding their purpose—*isn't* living, not only by Socrates' standards but also by Nature's.

Exclusive focus on forms and processes heightens complexity, which becomes more and more incomprehensible without a conceptual framework to keep all that detail organized and integrated. As a result, the "meaningless factor"—the "nonsense quotient"—increases as the system ages. Now you know why Scott Adams has an endless supply of material for *Dilbert*.

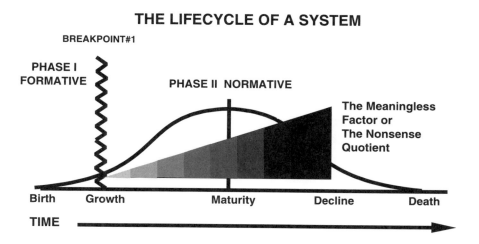

THE LIFECYCLE OF A SYSTEM

The normative phase confines thinking to linear, analytical processing—acquiring data and learning from authority: "This is how we do things around here". In an advanced, declining normative phase, we get the mindless Stimulus/Response mode that caused the psychologist B. F. Skinner to boast that, in an eighteen-month period, he could condition a human being to do almost anything. This is robot man, the completely mechanical perspective that sees only lists of facts and strings of data, with no clue to what they mean. It is conforming, unquestioning, un-critical, unexperimental, unchallenging—and mind-numbing boring. Here's a popular example of how mindless it gets:

> The U.S. Standard railroad gauge—the distance between the rails—is 4 feet, 8.5 inches—clearly not a "nice round number". Where did it come from? That was the gauge of English rail-roads. English expatriates built the first U.S. railroads. The people who built tramways—predecessors to railroads—built the first railroads in England. They used the same specifications they used for building wagons—4 feet, 8.5 inches between the wheels. The wagons used that odd spacing because the wheel ruts on the old long distance roads had that spacing. Who built those roads? The Romans. Roman war chariots made the ruts. The military spec for the wheel spacing on a Roman war chariot was ... 4 feet, 8.5 inches, of course. Why? Because that was just enough space to accommodate the rear end of two war horses. There-fore, U.S. railroads, today, are built to accommodate two, nine-teen-hundred-year-old horses' asses from Rome.

"Accommodating some horse's ass" really captures the essence of a nor-mative system. Now you know why so many people hate their bosses and have "problems with authority".

Dualism is the mechanism normative social institutions use to special-ize—to increase predictability. It causes the fragmentation that eventu-ally destroys them. Dualism is the practice of viewing the principal comple-ments of *any* system or subsystem as enemies rather than as partners in a larger whole. As such, it divides systems into progressively smaller, iso-lated antagonistic pieces until they become battlefields of tiny soldiers, each fighting for himself.

In Western history, for example, sectarianism first split the human race into the God-fearing versus the Heathen. The God-fearing created more antagonistic dualities: God against Satan, Heaven against Hell, Good against Evil, Man against Woman, spiritual against material. The God-fearing then split into Christians and Jews. Then the Christians split into

Protestants and Catholics. Then the Protestants divided into Lutherans, Congregationalists, Anglicans, Baptists, Methodists, and other denominations. See how it works? It literally is destruction. Think of dualism as a slow fission reaction in human social institutions.

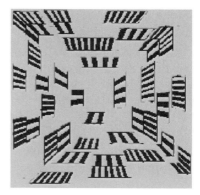

We see dualism in the thesis-antithesis dialectic of history, first described by Hegel. A revolution, an antithesis, rejects the established system *entirely*—its central principle, its processes, its forms. Therefore, the thesis that the revolutionaries oppose limits their own scope. The antithesis rejects *everything* in the domain of the thesis, no matter how valid it may be. That's why antagonistic revolutions—the only kind we can have in normative systems—can't produce true freedom. They can only build equal and opposite prisons that hold different people.

Dualism gives normative systems their "either-or" character: "Either you're with us or against us". Because they focus on form and process, normative systems say, "Either you look like us, you do things the way we do, or you don't. If you do, you're in. If you don't, you're out." When the system's objective is to reduce variance and increase predictability, deviance and diversity in both processes and people are "out"—very out.

In an old, declining normative system, antagonism toward deviation from "good form" becomes so petty that it's incomprehensible. Remember my accounts of Gaines™ Meal and the new package for Gaines™ Biscuits and Bits? It got even sillier. Shortly after those two incidents, I received a formal job evaluation. On the positive side, those two efforts, which *were* related to my competence, were cited as "nice tries". On the negative side, having no relation to my competence, were:

1) The trousers of my suits had no cuffs;

2) On occasion, I'd allowed my hair to reach my shirt collar before getting a haircut;

3) My shoes, while black, weren't wing tips;

4) I walked "funny". While other people dragged their feet and shuffled, I distinctly picked my feet up and put them down.

These issues, weighed against my competencies, produced the net evaluation: "Not management material". That looked to me like simple insanity at the time. Now I know what caused it. And remember, General Foods didn't live much longer after this.

The rules of normative systems are both formal and informal. The formal ones are written down as regulations, policies, and procedures. The informal controls, however, are usually more senseless, more powerful and more permanent. They exist as *memes*, a term coined by the brilliant biologist Richard Dawkins. Here's his definition:

> We need a name for the new replicator, a noun that conveys the idea of a unit of cultural transmission, or a unit of imitation. "Mimeme" comes from a suitable Greek root, but I want a monosyllable that sounds a bit like "gene." I hope my classicist friends will forgive me if I abbreviate mimeme to meme....

> Just as genes propagate themselves in the gene pool by leaping from body to body via sperms or eggs, so memes propagate themselves in the meme pool by leaping from brain to brain via a process which, in the broad sense, can be called imitation....

> As my colleague N. K. Humphrey neatly summed up "... memes should be regarded as living structures, not just metaphorically but technically. When you plant a fertile meme in my mind you literally parasitize my brain, turning it into a vehicle for the meme's propagation in just the way that a virus may parasitize the genetic mechanism of my host cell. And this isn't just a way of talking—the meme for say, 'belief in life after death' is actually realized, physically, millions of times over, as a structure in the nervous systems of individual men the world over."

Memes are the informal rules of normative cultures—broad institutions such as family, religion, business, and education, and the smaller cultures within them—individual families, denominations, companies, and schools.

Probably the most common and obvious way to enforce conformity is simply to ridicule a deviation, like a new idea, as silly, meaningless, stupid, crazy. But there are many more subtle memes in any normative culture. While he didn't use the term *meme*, Torrance, in his work on our educational system, gave names to the ones that annihilate creative thinking in children. They apply to school, the workplace, all social institutions. The only difference between schools and workplaces is the age of the participants.

Meme No. 1—Success Orientation

The title sounds positive. But rather than focusing on the primary causes of the desired result, as a formative system does, a normative system treats itself as the definition of "success". Under these conditions, "success orientation" means "Follow the rules—avoid negatives". A "negative", by definition, is anything that deviates from the system's tacit beliefs, its memes. Because a normative system assumes it already does all "the right things", to succeed is to conform and never ask why.

I once asked an organizational psychologist how he'd attempt to do new business development in an established company. He said:

> The first thing I'd do is locate the new business unit in Montana—in some town that's just about inaccessible—nowhere near an airport and a hell of a drive from anywhere. Then, I'd get one phone—just one—and screen incoming calls. The idea here is to quarantine yourself. You see, when you cut through all the motivational crap, there are only two primary motivations—pursuit of possibilities and avoidance of negatives. New business is about pursuing possibilities. Around 3 percent of our population does that. About 92 percent are completely concerned with avoiding negatives. There's a 5 percent swing group that is sometimes motivated by one, sometimes by the other. As a company ages, it first throws out the obvious "pursue possibilities" types. Then it gets rid of those who *might* pursue possibilities. Those left devoutly avoid negatives. They pose no threat of introducing diversity, and they have sworn to kill off any who do—like you and your new business unit, for instance.

I came to call this avoidance of deviation, diversity, and negative consequences "life in a minefield". People spend their time and energy figuring out how to avoid getting blown up. Picture, for a minute, a life almost entirely composed of decisions about how to *avoid* negative consequences—a life about what *not* to do. This is the *normal* view of life. How *could* anyone find meaning in it?

Meme No. 2—Peer Orientation

All memes in normative systems directly or indirectly enforce external dependency. This one demonstrates that very clearly. "Peer orientation" is normality's benchmark. It says, "The majority opinion is the right opinion. To know what is right, find out what most people think." All we know for sure about the majority opinion is that it is almost never the best answer. But notice how it answers a qualitative issue quantitatively? That's more obsession with the material to the exclusion of the spiritual—form and process without purpose.

Growth, change, and progress don't come from majority rule. Everett Rogers broke new ground when he studied how innovations are actually adopted. He found that the "new" is created by "Innovators", the 2.5 percent of any normally distributed population who have the personal strength to be minorities of one. On a bell curve, they are +3 standard deviations from the mean, from "normal". They are *major* deviants. Innovations first move to "Early Adopters". These are people who think more independently than most. They are not totally committed to the status quo. They look for ways to make things work better. They are the first ones to try any new solution that holds promise. When they find one that works, they adopt it. That, in effect, endorses it to the balance of the population, the "Early Majority" and the "Late Majority". Once

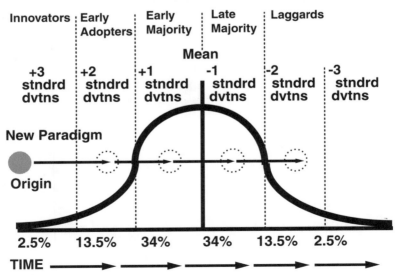

THE ADOPTION OF CHANGE IN SOCIAL SYSTEMS

that happens, it's O.K. for "normal" people to do it this way, because it has become "the way we do things around here".

Realize that "normal" people do not adopt innovation because they make an independent, thoughtful evaluation of it. They are imitators. Their lives are about things that are "approved". This is what external dependence is all about. Normal people avoid the risk of making a mistake, which might occur if they thought for themselves. Now ask yourself, "How can a person who will not think for himself or herself find meaning in life?" Obviously, being confined to forms and processes, the *mechanics* of life, that person can't. Being "normal" and finding meaning in life are mutually exclusive. To "be normal" is not a goal of life. It's a goal of machinery.

"Normal" is that wasteland where people believe they are avoiding negative consequences by carefully following the system's norms. They're partially right. Negative consequences are imposed on those who deviate from the system's norms by those who swore to uphold them—The Early and Late Majority. These are the status quo police. They are externally dependent themselves. They force external dependency and extrinsic motivation on others. These are the functionaries, people who perform required actions with no knowledge of their purpose. In any social institution, the chief functionary is typically its head—the head of the church, the head of state. In most companies, it's the CEO. Enforcing conformity to the norms is top management's real job. People become top management precisely because they are the most aggressively loyal conformists. If you've heard of "the cloning factor" in corporations, now you know what it means. Of course most top managers have no vision. If they did, they wouldn't be top managers. They fear vision and creativity, no matter what buzzwords they preach.

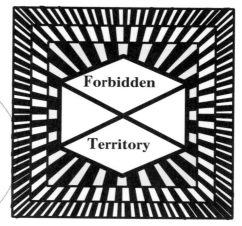

Under the rule of the status quo police, the system's original spiritual state is forbidden territory.

Let's be very clear about this. Normative systems impose a view of life on the people in them that includes only material states—forms and processes. This *denies people access to meaning which denies them the right to their own spiritual existence.* This is true of any normative system, regardless of the area of life it controls—government, education, law, business, or religion. Perhaps the infantry soldiers of the U.S. Army described normalcy best—"Ours is not to wonder why. Ours is but to do—and die."

Meme No. 3—Sanctions against Questioning and Exploring

Kids intuitively seek meaning. They ask, "Why?" Their parents, who've learned not to ask that question, teach their children not to ask it. In the process, they unwittingly drive their kids into a meaningless existence. They get a lot of help from teachers, principals, priests, ministers, rabbis, and other adults. Two of the more popular admonitions against asking "why?" that I remember from my childhood, were "Curiosity killed the cat" and, "When you're older, you'll understand". If you've ever asked *why* your company had some particular practice, I'll bet the answer you got was, "Because that's the way we do it around here." It means, "I don't know why and don't ask!"

Meme No. 4—Gender Jail

Perhaps the most discussed polarity in any society is the difference between male and female. Yet Torrance points out:

> Creativity, by its very nature, requires both sensitivity and independence. In our culture, sensitivity is definitely a feminine virtue, while independence is a masculine value.

What could be a more intimidating way to discourage creativity and independent thought than by accusing a person, especially a child, of violating his/her gender? Remember, gender is the *primary* means, in our normative culture, of affirming a person's existence. The first question we all ask upon hearing of a newborn baby is, "Is it a boy or a girl?"

Yet in *Creativity: Flow and the Psychology of Discovery and Invention*, Mihaly Csikszentmihalyi describes how comfortable creative people are with their own paradoxical traits—characteristics "normally" considered mutually exclusive. Creative people are *both* highly energetic and quiet and peaceful. They are both smart and naive, playful and disciplined, extroverted and introverted, humble and proud, conservative and rebellious, passionate and objective. They are equally comfortable with convergent and divergent thinking, with fantasy and reality, with things intangible and things tangible, with both spiritual and material states. These people are definitely *not* "normal". They're *integrative*.

Meme No. 5—Equating Divergency with Mental Illness, Perversity or Evil

Normative systems warn that any divergence from their tacit beliefs is unhealthy and sick. It must be cured. Children are taught very early that to be different is to be bad, inferior, even mentally ill. When someone applies this view to an entire group of people, we call it bigotry. Yet the protectors of the status quo constantly apply it to creative, integrative individuals to prevent the inquisitive thinking that might challenge and dislodge established memes.

Meme No. 6—The Dichotomy between Work and Play

I discovered this one when I was a kid. I called it the "Castor Oil Syndrome." If you enjoy something, if it's fun, it's bad for you—it's worthless. Conversely, if you hate it, it's good for you—it's worthwhile. It "builds character". Play is fun; therefore, it's "bad". Work is "castor oil". It's good for us because we dislike it so much. What was this nonsense? Well, I first heard it in church. It's one of the core neuroses of our Puritan/Judeo-Christian heritage. If we really enjoy something, it's not worth any redemption points with the Big Scorekeeper in the Sky. Do we hate work simply because we've been convinced that it must be joyless to be worthwhile? Do you suppose there might be some correlation between hating work and not finding meaning in it?

Human systems originated to solve problems, to improve mankind's well-being. But normative systems are the ultimate Catch-22s. Because they can't adapt, they must perpetuate the problem they were established to solve in order to perpetuate their own existence. Without "Original Sin", for example, Christianity has no reason for being. Most psychological therapy doesn't advocate self-actualization. It advocates normality, which guarantees its practitioners an endless supply of neuroses.

The two columns below summarize the traits of the formative and normative phases of social institutions. Because normative systems are "either-or" in nature, they adhere to the traits on the right, excluding and punishing those on the left.

FORMATIVE	NORMATIVE
spiritual	material
soul	body
theory	fact
design	structure
synthetical	analytical
intangible	tangible
holistic	fragmented
see	do
function	form
right-brained	left-brained
qualitative	quantitative
diverse	homogenous
distinctive	commoditized
inclusive	exclusive
people in charge of the system	system in charge of the people
creative learning	learning by authority

The Integrative Phase

The integrative phase means unifying the fragments of the normative phase by recognizing *both* the spiritual and material states of a system, *both* its principal complements and its original purpose. It doesn't mean throwing away what exists. It means discovering the meaning behind it. It often requires redesigning the system, based on its original intent, to fit current conditions.

An integrative system recognizes both its spiritual and material states.

The integrative phase is an *open, adaptive* system. It resolves the Catch-22s we see in the normative phase. People know the system's original purpose—its *Why*. An integrative system is like H_2O in its liquid state, water. It recognizes both its spiritual and material states and continually flows back and forth between them. Because it is tightly linked to its other principal complement in its environment, it adapts its forms and processes to external changes. It is fluid rather than rigid.

If you understand the difference between the formative and normative phases of a system, understanding the integrative phase is easy. Integrate the formative and normative, the spiritual and the material, and you get a whole system.

People in open, integrative systems continue to acknowledge the system's origin, its two principal complements, and its intent. They understand the basis of unity between the principal complements, even after the system has become large and materially complex. Therefore, they can see the *meaning* behind its forms and processes. They can see the relationships between causes and effects. They know *why* things do or don't make sense. They know what to change and when it needs to be changed. Unlike within a normative system, whose complexity is incomprehensible, people can comfortably function in the complexity of an integrative system because they have the foundation of *purpose* for organizing all the details.

In an integrative or open, adaptive system, people practice *inclusion* of diversity rather than *exclusion*. They transcend dualism. That keeps the system integrated even after it is concretely complex. They are concerned with both function and form because they focus on how things are complementary, how they "fit together". They remember that their goal is to accomplish the system's original intent. Subsystems evolve interdependently rather than independently.

We have many examples of open, adaptive, integrative systems in nature. Ant and bee colonies are two of the more popular ones. But any ecosystem, no matter how you define it, is a complex of interdependent open, adaptive systems.

Within the realm of human experience, there are many examples of systems that *began* as open systems—in business, in government (democracy, the founding philosophy of the U.S. government), and in education. But an integrative system remains open and adaptive after it is fully operational. By this criteria, the only examples of ongoing, integrative systems that I know of are specific people. Integrative people:

1. Have a sense of purpose for their own lives;

2. Are grounded in the originating purpose of whatever system they work in;

3. Are keenly focused on "the other" principal complement;

4. Work toward the reconciliation of antagonistic separation, the re-unification of parts into wholes. They live to unify.

Consider Abraham Lincoln. Although he became president long after our originally open system of government had entered its closed, normative phase, he himself was grounded in its original purpose—a government "of the people, by the people, and for the people".

Albert Einstein was one of history's preeminent integrative thinkers. Fritjof Capra, a physicist who wrote *The Turning Point*, elegantly portrayed the integrative view when he said, "At the rate we're going, physics will prove spirituality". If you know John Lennon's music or his writings, you know that he, too, was an integrative. The *Tao Teh King* (also *Tao Te Ching*) by Lao Tzu is a complete work devoted to transcending dualism into unity. Socrates, also, was an integrative.

The best-known integrative in Western culture was Jesus Christ. I'm referring only to the man, not to the social institutions that co-opted his name to perpetuate the same normative, dualistic antagonism he transcended. At church, I heard two very different definitions of God. Most often, God was portrayed as the Supreme Being, the ultimate judge in the battle between good and evil. This was a God to fear. Once in a while, I'd hear that "God is love", "God is unity", "God is one", meaning the unified whole of life. I knew these definitions contradicted one another. Now I know why. The first is not only God in man's image, it's God in man's *normative* image. The second is the integrative view of God. Therefore, an integrative person is one who is "made in God's image".

Science has been a bit more tolerant of integratives than other areas of society. Integrative thinking in a normative world has often literally been a matter of life or death.

The ninety-one people Csikszentmihalyi interviewed for his book *Creativity: Flow and the Psychology of Discovery and Innovation* are undoubtedly integratives. They've made significant contributions in many different fields. They've come from many countries. But they all had one thing in common: they all had a specific purpose, pursued it, and accomplished it. Their work had meaning to others, but it had great meaning to them *first*. They didn't do it for recognition. They weren't *externally* motivated. They did it because they saw an opportunity to make things work better that was meaningful to them. They were *internally* motivated. In Joseph Campbell's words, integrative people are those whose *"life experiences on the purely physical plane... have resonance within* [their] *own innermost being and reality, so that* [they] *actually feel the rapture of being alive."*

Creativity, purpose, meaning, spirit, origin, art, authenticity, integrity, unity, and the sense of being fully alive are inextricably linked.

I learned the following exercise from George Land. It allows people actually to experience the difference between a normative and an integrative perspective. Following is a list of word pairs. Create two sentences using each pair. First, place the words "either" and "or" between the words. For example, "A person's opinion is either factual or intuitive." Then, using the same sentence, place "both" and "and" between the words, such as, "A person's opinion is both factual and intuitive."

Conforming—Deviant	Following—Leading
Factual—Intuitive	Linear—Pictorial
Concrete—Abstract	Material—Spiritual
Known—Unknown	Tactical—Strategic

How does each make you feel? Notice how the normative version ("either-or") allows you to put the subject of the sentence in one box or the other and close the box, while the integrative version ("both-and") doesn't. If there is a box in your view of the integrative, at least it's an open box. The normative version separates; it's exclusive. The integrative version unites; it's inclusive.

If you've come across Eastern religions, you've probably heard paradoxical statements such as, "To have it all, you have to give it all up". Viktor Frankl, who wrote *Man's Search for Meaning*, founded Logotherapy. Logos is a Greek word that denotes meaning. Therefore, "Logotherapy" means correcting an absence of meaning in one's life or, a process for finding meaning. Its principal technique is "paradoxical intention". If you've never seen this term before, what does it probably mean? How about "the reconciliation of apparent opposites through a common intention". And what is that? It's the definition of the origin of an *open* system—where its *meaning* is.

Understanding integrative systems allows us to understand why "paradoxical intention" works. It moves the person's focus away from tangible effects to intangible, originating cause. It reconciles antagonistic principal complements. Remember Christ's "Love thy enemy"? Different words, same meaning. "Paradoxical intention" and "Love thy enemy" mean embracing what the person rejects or, more accurately, fears. It transcends duality into unity and fills the void of meaning. This raises an interesting question. Do you suppose that, by "Heaven", Christ meant a life *with* meaning and, that "Hell" is a life *without* it?

Summary

All systems, whether natural or man-made, begin as intangible designs. They have a purpose that unifies their principal complements. We can understand the origins of man-made systems. The true origin of natural systems is still unknown—regardless of

	Open	Closed
Formative	Man-made (and Natural?)	Man-made and Natural
Normative		Man-made
Integrative	Natural (and Man-made?)	

what science and theology claim to know. The formative phase translates a system's spiritual state into its material state. Those that fit well with their environment survive and prosper. Those that don't, don't.

Systems can originate as open or closed, but the majority of both natural and man-made systems appear to originate as closed systems. Once viable, however, man-made systems and natural systems develop very differently.

Natural systems may prosper for tens or hundreds of thousands of years because they are naturally open, adaptive, integrated systems, even though their design *may* have occurred by accident. (The concept of purposeful evolution challenges the traditional view that evolution occurs randomly. The traditional definition may be due more to normative thinking than to reality. We've yet to answer that one.)

Man-made systems, including social institutions, from individual businesses to entire societies, become normative, closed systems. At least in the Western world, their maximum life span is rarely more than a few hundred years. Most don't live that long. Organized religions are exceptions to that rule. Many have lasted thousands of years. But remember, they are often about a next life, not this one. Their founding hypothesis can't be tested. If there is no next life, who's going to tell us?

Because they deny the spiritual state—originating cause—normative systems produce the Catch-22s that make life senseless and meaningless. Being normal means living a life that has no meaning to the person living it. The solution is quite literally to change our view of reality—to move forward into an open, integrative view of it. This is extremely difficult, primarily because it's more about unlearning old stuff than about learning new stuff. To put a new engine in a car, you first have to remove the old one. In the U.S., as in any culture, we've all been subjected to thousands of memes that come from a normative view of reality. Before we get into the deeply personal issues of moving from a normative to an integrative perspective, let's look at the memes we'll have to unlearn in the United States, and where they came from.

*I know of no country, indeed, where the love of money has
taken stronger hold on the affections of men.*

—Alexis De Tocqueville, *Democracy in America*

Chapter Four

*How We Got Where We Are
Today in the USA*

When we think of the United States of America, we think of it as an
entirely new culture because it created a new form of government—
a republic without a monarch, governed by elected officials, which we call a
"democracy". Its form of government originated as an open system. It clearly
recognized the other principal complement—the citizens. Its originating
purpose integrated the well-being of the individual citizen with the prosper-
ity of the collective society. U.S. citizens have greater freedom to live according to their personal beliefs than people in most cultures. But those
beliefs created our culture, not our form of government. A culture's beliefs
come from "memes"—mentally transmitted units of imitation passed from
generation to generation. Most of the memes by which this culture still lives
were brought over from Europe 400 years ago, when the New World was
first settled.

Our system of beliefs was formed by the convergence of three social
movements in England and Europe in the sixteenth and early seventeenth centuries—the rise of Protestantism and, more specifically, an
English version of it, Puritan Protestantism; the Scientific Revolution,
and mercantilism.

Puritan Protestantism

By the beginning of the sixteenth century, the Roman Catholic Church had a long history of condemning man's material existence. Its condemnation of commerce was rooted in the biblical injunction in Deuteronomy against usury—profiting by lending money. The story of Jesus chasing the money changers out of the Temple reinforced it. St. Paul added more fuel to the fire when he wrote to Timothy:

> If we have food and clothing, we shall be content. But those who desire to be rich fall into temptation, into a snare, into many senseless and hurtful desires that plunge men into ruin and destruction. For the love of money is the root of all evils; it is through this craving that some have wandered away from the faith and pierced their hearts with many pangs. (1 Timothy 6:8–10.)

St. Paul linked money to material existence and sin. By the sixteenth century, the Roman Catholic Church had banned military and government personnel, carpenters, stucco-workers, cabinet workers, thatchers, gold-leaf beaters, bronze workers, engravers, dealers in meat and flowers and, above all, traders and bankers, from its sanctuaries. If you couldn't live by theology alone, you were headed for Hell and not wanted in the Church. This thesis begged for an antithesis. It got it, both from within and without.

In 1517 Martin Luther nailed his Ninety-five Theses, challenging the Church's practices to the rectory door. In 1529, the Catholic majority of German rulers prohibited Luther's teaching. A group of his supporters protested the decision and were labeled "Protestants". In 1533 King Henry VIII of England, looking for an excuse to divorce his first wife, broke with the pope and formed the Anglican Church.

In 1536 John Calvin, godfather of the Puritans who would sail to Massachusetts in 1630, published *Institutes of the Christian Religion*. Because the ban on usury was in the Old Testament, Calvin contended it applied only to Hebrews. In 1638, a Dutch Calvinist named Claude Saumaise came out in *favor* of usury, claiming it was actually necessary for salvation. England, where the Puritans would execute King Charles I and seize power in 1649, became the first nation to approve lending with interest. The acquisition of wealth was acquiring theological support. Money was, for the first time, "righteous". It not only provided power over men; it became the sign that one was headed for the Pearly

Gates. The Calvinist Puritans reversed Christ's view that "it is easier for a camel to pass through the eye of a needle than for a rich man to enter the kingdom of heaven." According to them, getting rich was God's proof in a predestined world that you were going to Heaven. If you weren't rich, you weren't going.

In 1697 John Locke wrote: "Riches do not consist in having more gold and silver, but in having more in proportion than the rest of the world, or than our neighbors. Our growing rich depends only on which is greater or less, our importation or exportation of consumable commodities." By making wealth relative, Locke and Protestantism made it the basis of social hierarchy.

A reversal in Protestant theology about the relationship between poverty and sin further reinforced God's smile upon those who make money. During the reign of Queen Elizabeth I (1558–1603), most English people believed that weaknesses in the economic system caused poverty. By the 1670s, however, the Puritans began to assert that poverty was caused by sin, especially lust and laziness. Conversely, worldly success demonstrated virtue. Now, Puritan Protestantism fully supported a social hierarchy based on accumulated wealth—in opposition to Roman Catholicism's official position at the time.

The Puritan Protestants said, in effect "If you want to get to Heaven, wealth is THE thing." And they were far more committed to correct forms, processes, and practices—the classic traits of normative systems—than they were to the principles behind them. As the historian Perry Miller wrote in *Errand into the Wilderness*, "The Puritans were devotees of logic, and the verb 'methodize' ruled their thinking." We're about to see why.

Cartesian Science: Mechanism and Materialism

What we call the Scientific Revolution was the external, secular revolution against the Roman Catholic Church. It allied with the internal revolution and deepened the split between the material and the spiritual.

The Church asserted its omniscience. It claimed to know everything about everything because it was so intimately connected to God, the source of everything. Based on its views of human origins, it deduced the nature of reality. One of the Church's deductions was that the Sun revolved around the Earth. Copernicus brought the Church's credibility into question with his discovery that, in fact, the reverse was true. A new science gushed forth, alongside the new view of wealth. Descartes and Sir Isaac Newton wrote its catechism.

Like all traditional revolutionaries, these early scientists took a position diametrically opposed to the existing thesis. The Church's position was that only the spiritual, the (literally speaking) immaterial, was "good" and the corporeal, the material, was "bad". The equal and opposite position of the new scientists was that truth—reality—could be found *only* in the material. As far as they were concerned, "Only matter matters". Implicit in this view was that the more tangible something is, the more real, or true, it is. That's why, today, we still equate "reality" with the material state of things. According to these revolutionaries, "meaning" existed *only* in the material.

René Descartes defined the character of the Scientific Revolution with his twenty-one rules for "how to think". Descartes was educated by Jesuits, who actively supported the sciences but taught in Aristotelian logic. Aristotle's view began with purpose, the reason something existed in the first place. From that, its nature, composition, capabilities, and *modus operandi* all were deduced, showing *how* the thing accomplishes its purpose. In *Descartes: An Intellectual Biography*, Stephen Gaukroger described Aristotle's perspective as "resembling the ripples caused by throwing a stone into a pond, which spread out and combine with the ripples caused by other stones." Aristotle saw systems.

Descartes took on both Aristotle and his Jesuit teachers. Rather than start with an intangible principle and deduce the effects it would produce (spiritual state to material state) Descartes wanted to work back from final effects to cause. He referred to this as having a "clear and distinct idea". By "idea", he didn't mean a mind's eye image. He meant its simplest, most isolated, most tangible *form*. He prescribed what we now call linear, sequential, analytical, "left-brain" thinking—thinking confined to forms and processes. This is "Cartesian reductionism".

Descartes' twenty-one rules prohibited Aristotle's teleological thinking— the actualization of essence or purpose—because that's how the Church had arrived at its obviously spurious knowledge of "reality". Discrediting both the process and the results, Descartes labeled Aristotle's way "the sterile demonstrations of the ancients". Over time, Descartes got progressively more liberal about how tangible something had to be, to be considered "matter". Eventually, he asserted that life itself is just a series of events. As they evolved in practice, his rules for how to think scientifically prevented any search for meaning, much less the ability to actually find it. They prohibited the mental processes necessary to have Aha!s, Eureka!s, and epiphanies—the ability to "get it" that discloses meaning.

Descartes' approach meshed perfectly with Puritan "methodizing". Less than 150 years after his *Discourse on Method*, the two would show up, blended, in the about-to-be United States, as Benjamin Franklin constructed the first Franklin Organizer for methodically measuring his performance on thirteen moral virtues.

As a challenge to the Church's dictatorial play of omniscience, which controlled people through nearly unassailable mythology, the Scientific Revolution was a noble, enlightening, and freeing endeavor. But in defining matter as the source of meaning, it was just plain *wrong*. In deifying parts to the exclusion of wholes, it created massive confusion and a profound departure from reality. Cartesian thinking made meaning impossible to find. It epitomized the normative, valuing tangible, material effects to the exclusion of their intangible, spiritual causes.

Cartesian thinking began in the sciences. Thanks to Einstein and the rise of chaos and complexity theory (complex systems, general systems) it's now on its way out. During the interim, however, it spread throughout our society, especially our educational system. Harvard is a good example. Harvard College was founded—for the purpose of training Puritan ministers—just six years after the Massachusetts Bay Colony was settled. One hundred seventy years later, the Harvard School of Business was founded to further the scientific management theories of Frederick Taylor. Taylorism epitomizes the isolated specialization of a normative system, assigning each worker a specific task and preventing the others from knowing what he or she does. Taylor had applied Cartesian reductionism—mechanical process control—to people.

Our institutions of higher learning still teach this kind of thinking. Consider these two accounts from *Creativity: Flow and the Psychology of Discovery and Invention* by Mihaly Csikszentmihalyi. The first is of Gerald Holton, a physicist who later became a science historian. He was a graduate student at Harvard "immersed in the heady atmosphere of logical positivism", which is to say that science can be reduced to pure logic, prohibiting anything that might be considered intuitive or metaphysical.

But Holton, reading about scientific luminaries such as Kepler and Einstein, realized that this approach did not apply to scientific break-throughs, new discoveries of *meaning*.

The other account is by Barry Commoner, a biophysicist, teacher, and activist who left academia to confront problems such as the quality of water and the disposal of garbage:

> The prevailing philosophy in academic life is [Cartesian] reduc-tionism, which is exactly the reverse of my approach to things, and I'm not interested in doing it.

Holton and Commoner had to break with the way people are still trained to think, today, to achieve their goals. Both rejected the normative per-spective for the integrative.

Puritan Protestantism and Cartesian science, combined with mercantil-ism, formed the dominant institution in American society—business, as played by the rules we title "capitalism".

Mercantilism

In the sixteenth century, the Spanish and the Portuguese looted the cities of the Aztecs and the Incas. Some of the gold and silver they brought back flooded the European economy, causing rampant inflation. The rest was stockpiled as war chests. England came late to the Americas and found no wealthy natives to exploit, so it determined to become rich another way.

England had no precious metals, but it did have an industrious popula-tion. Most of its output was fabric, which was made into clothes and household products. Mercantilism became the queen's alchemy for turn-ing fabric into gold.

The purpose of mercantilism was to accumulate wealth. Mercantilism sought to create an imbalance of trade in favor of the seller. If England exported more than it imported, it could claim the difference in gold or silver. The queen said, "Buy a little, sell a lot, show me the gold." The more favorable trading England could do, the faster it could accumulate wealth.

Mercantilism discarded the two *living* principals in the business transaction—the *beneficiaries* of the exchange: producer and user—for two inanimate *media* of exchange: goods and money. This obliterated the *spirit* of the exchange. It recognized only its quantitative, material character.

Mercantilism also made the exchange adversarial by requiring favorable (im)balances of trade. It's no secret where the "win-lose" attitude of American business comes from. Furthermore, mercantilism treated goods as commodities because its primary focus was on gold and silver, the ultimate commodities.

To implement her scheme for accumulating wealth, the queen needed more distributors, merchants, and acquirers. She found them.

Throughout feudal times, England's landowning nobles were men of leisure. Their income came from renting out their land to tenant farmers through agreements, fixed in perpetuity, between their families and those of the tenants. Primogeniture meant that a man's first-born son inherited the entire estate, but it could usually support the younger sons as well. When the Spanish and Portuguese precious metals wrought rampant inflation in England, the gentry could not, by the terms of the agreements, raise rents to compensate. Their life of leisure plummeted. The younger sons were sent to the cities to earn their keep. That was tough in an age of craft; they didn't have one. Their skills were drinking, wenching, hunting foxes and, maybe, reading, writing, and a little arithmetic. But they were fueled by desperation.

In those days, "birthright"—the situation into which a child was born—determined one's purpose in life. Daughters had the purpose of raising children and caring for husbands and households. The sons of tradesmen and craftsmen had the purpose of carrying on the family trade. The eldest sons of the gentry had the purpose of managing the family estate. But these younger sons were born into lives of effects they didn't cause and weren't required to perpetuate. They were born to lives that had no inherent purpose. They were born to normality. But now they needed a new place to apply it.

The queen needed warm bodies to move goods from producers to users, to receive goods exchanged for them, to keep records, especially of the amount of gold to be collected. The required job skills were arrogance, fast mouths, foolhardiness, and a little arithmetic, reading, and writing. These kids were made for it. They had the skills and shared the queen's goal—to accumulate wealth. They wanted their lifestyle back. Suddenly, they were more than just merchants. The queen gave them a purpose. They became the soldiers of the queen's economic army. England's merchant class was the fountainhead of win-lose exchanges conducted to accumulate wealth. They shared in their success. The most successful became rich, important, politically powerful men. Does all this seem more recent than 400 years ago?

This bit of history fascinated me. First, I'd found that mercantilism is the root of America's concept of business. Second, I've met these second-sons-of-the-landed-gentry kids throughout my career. They usually have an Ivy League M.B.A and work in either marketing or finance, especially venture capital. They all look like the actors Cary Elwes or Hugh Grant. Scott Adams captured their mentality in this *Dilbert* strip:

DILBERT reprinted by permission of United Media Syndicate, Inc.

I'd found their foundation stock. Consider a lifestyle that constantly searches for the "right things"—where to live, what car to drive, what restaurants to eat at, what country clubs to belong to, what clothes to wear, and whom to know. This is the archetype of the normative person—thoroughly externally dependent, with a perspective confined to material existence. These are the Aha!-less.

It's no accident that the Boston area is their homeland. It is the cultural bedrock of the northern United States. The Massachusetts Bay Company's settlement team arrived in 1630. It was much more than a company. It was a colony, a complete social organism. While the surface of history celebrates these colonists as noble seekers of religious freedom, their motives were as much or more economic. It was a consummately normative system when it arrived. Its civil government, as Perry Miller wrote in *Errand into the Wilderness*, had:

...at the very beginning of its list of responsibilities, the duty of suppressing heresy, of subduing or somehow getting rid of dissenters—of being, in short, deliberately, vigorously, and consistently intolerant.

Our predominant structure for conducting business also came from England. Joint stock companies, in which investors pooled capital to fund some undertaking, existed as early as 1407, when the English government officially recognized the aptly named Merchant Adventurers. This was the form of venture capital that funded the East India Company, the Virginia Company, and the Massachusetts Bay Company. Unlike a guild, it was legally recognized as its own entity, independent of specific people. In *The English People on the Eve of Colonization*, the historian Wallace Notestein wrote:

> The new companies affected English life. The hope of making money quickly, as Drake had done...induced merchants to buy shares in every new company organized and drew in as investors many of the nobility and gentry. They forgot the enormous losses undergone and remembered the few successes.

We're still using this structure in the United States today. It's "the corporation".

Mercantilism was also a nurturing environment for the Industrial Revolution. Machines increased productivity. More goods meant more "favorable trades". Inventories were seen as piles of gold. No one stopped to consider whether or not a market for them existed. As Thomas Mun put it: "The main thing is to possess goods; if you have them, you will get money. He that hath ware, hath money by the year." And remember Locke's view: "Our growing rich depends only on which is greater or less, our importation or exportation of consumable commodities."

Combine industrial manufacturing with the joint stock company and you get the archetype of American business—the manufacturing corporation. This entity believes its purpose is to accumulate wealth. It treats its products as undifferentiated commodities. The original emphasis on providing investors with a return is the primary reason so many of today's CEOs still say their first responsibility is to the company's [often uninvolved and virtually unknown] stockholders, even though American companies produce goods and services for markets of users rather than going on treasure hunts for the queen.

Adam Smith's primary contribution to all this was that he helped move the mercantilist corporation out from under government control and put it in the hands of the citizenry. That occasioned a name change from "mercantilism" to "capitalism".

As Sir Isaac Newton founded the science of physics, so Adam Smith may be said to have founded the science of economics. Unfortunately, he was working in the late eighteenth century when mercantilism, Protestantism, and Cartesian mechanism were all the rage. He assumed, as do most people in American companies today, that "economics" and "business" are synonymous. They're not. Economics is actually the formal quantification of mercantilism. It tracks the movement of money and aggregate volumes of goods. It treats goods and services as undifferentiated commodities. It is concerned only with the results produced by the material state of business. It has no concern for their causes—*why* the movements occur. How many times have you heard someone attempt to explain a business with, "Well, you know, it's all just basic supply and demand." Translated, that means, "I haven't got the foggiest idea what this business is really about or why it works."

Like Descartes, Newton, and Franklin, Smith was a mechanist. He objected to mercantilism only because he objected to government control of trade. He'd become fascinated by a pin factory. Each worker was an expert in one minuscule part of making a pin. Anticipating Taylor by 100 years, he noted that this specialization produced many more pins each day than a craft guild, where each worker made the whole product. Each pin cost less, too. Smith concluded that cost per unit decreased as volume increased. To assure the lowest price, the market had to continually expand to absorb increasing supply. He saw government control as the limiting factor in this scheme. Smith answered those who challenged the stability of a free-trade system by stating that the individual "is led by the invisible hand of the marketplace to promote an end which was no part of his [original] intention". Smith's "invisible hand" was his glimpse of the other principal complement in the business transaction—the user. For a fleeting instant, he saw the key dualist flaw in mercantilism. In *The Wealth of Nations*, Smith wrote:

> Consumption is the sole end and purpose of all production; and the interest of the producer ought to be attended to, only so far as it may be necessary for promoting that of the consumer. That maxim is so perfectly self-evident that it would be absurd to at-

tempt to prove it. But in the mercantile system, the interest of the consumer is almost constantly sacrificed to that of the producer; and it seems to consider production, and not consumption, as the end and object of all industry and commerce.

Smith apparently never recognized the significance of what he'd written. His primary focus was volumetric—quantitative, not qualitative. He never asked *why* producers ignore consumers and what effect that has. Therefore, he was never in a position to create a science of business—only the mechanics of economics. This is what most American companies still think is "business".

Economics is only a record of aggregated final *effects* of mercantilist exchanges—a completely normative view that includes only the objects of exchange—goods and money. It excludes the people who benefit from the exchanges—the *cause* of the transactions. "Capitalism"—the American Dream—is simply mercantilist economics in the hands of citizens rather than the government. Most American companies don't manage businesses. They govern economies. They have no conception of the whole system—*business*.

Remember Pillsbury's top management's reaction to my proposal that we deliberately create products that help users do what they're trying to do?: "That's not the way it's done." Well, now you know why they had that reaction. Unexamined memes really do parasitize people's minds.

Summary

"The accumulation of wealth is the road to heaven" was the core of Puritan Protestantism. "Life is just a series of events" and "Only matter matters" were the core of Cartesian science. Mercantilism made the pursuit of wealth the core purpose of the United States' socio-economic system. Cartesian reductionism taught us to think in bits and pieces rather than in wholes.

This is a very large portion of the cultural foundation of the United States of America.

Collectively, Puritan Protestantism, Cartesian science, and mercantilism greatly increased emphasis on material existence, on pieces, and on form. This amounts to "revolutionary" *intensification of normalizing*—a giant leap forward *on the same path* inaugurated by the rise of civilization, itself. That journey has progressed relatively undisturbed in the U.S. compared to Europe. Therefore, we can say that the U.S., as it enters the twenty-first century, is the crowning achievement of seventeenth-century Europe.

This potentially paralyzing confinement has been alleviated in the U.S. by an open, integrative philosophy of government that permitted greater freedom of the individual—specifically, of the individual's mind.

The net effect is a society in which most of its members can see only that part of life where meaning *doesn't exist*. But the U.S. also provides a supportive environment for those who want to reclaim their ability to find meaning. Our form of social control is more tolerant of deviation— more supportive of the individual's right to think independently and creatively. That's why, for example, Americans, in general, look like "wild cards" to the Japanese. In other words, along with this black hole of normative memes that constitute American culture comes greater permission to challenge them. That's the work of the individual person.

Part II

The Person

Only people can see meaning. Only people can create systems based on purpose and include others in those systems by communicating that meaning. The ability to do these things requires *being* integrative. Given the culture of the United States, most of us need to *become* integrative to find meaning. And becoming integrative is mostly about *un-learning* "being normal".

The previous chapter described some of the false notions inherent in our culture. Those are *what* to unlearn. The hard part is *how* to unlearn—developing the ability actually to do it. Unlearning is far more difficult than learning, especially when you realize that we acquired much of what we need to unlearn when we were very young children. For example, my grandmother, with whom we lived, was a devout bigot. Fortunately for me, my father was not, so her bigotry never got an exclusive hold on my subconscious. Even so, I found some stereotypical views of races and nationalities in my subconscious. I had simply absorbed them from my home environment at around four or five years of age. I had to "unlearn" them in my thirties.

Psychologists call this process "peeling your own onion". It's an accurate metaphor. Unlearning requires examining what you believe. Is it functional? Does it make things work, or does it make things *not* work? Then, examine its source. Is the source functional? If not, then find its source—and so on and so on. We're literally peeling away layers and layers of normative memes—those belief viruses that parasitize our minds. At each layer, the person must make a decision to keep the belief or throw it away.

Actually removing a meme from the subconscious is very difficult. I found I not only had to identify the belief but also relive the *emotion* hooked to it, and bring the entire package into current reality, in order to let it go. The emotion most often hooked to a belief is fear—fear of the negative consequences of *not* believing it. Facing that fear makes removing a meme a nasty process.

People acquire most of their beliefs subtly. We are infected simply by being immersed in seas of memes in the minds around us. That makes finding their source tricky. It requires great ability to focus, to probe our own *normal* experiences, not our acute traumas. It helps to realize that, when the goal is to find meaning, "normal" means *dysfunctional*, not functional.

People often feel there's no end to the process. They peel off one layer and find more inaccurate, delusional, dysfunctional beliefs underneath. That gets tiring. But there is an end to it. And there are rewards along the way. They come in the form of revelations—the Aha!s of deeper insight into what's really going on. These make the journey tolerable and, sometimes, outright exhilarating.

The next two chapters lay bare the dysfunctional effects imposed on people by normative systems. They provide the means to consciously recognize the undesirability of what we've been conditioned to desire.

The leadership systems currently in place too often look at us as our doing, as they say do differently in order to change. But the Indian way says we're not human doings, we're human beings. If we want to change the doing in leadership, I need to change my being. And the way to change my being is to change my intent.

—Don Coylis, Mohican, 1993. Quoted in *Native American Visions*, a 1998 calendar published by American Indian Science and Engineering Society.

Chapter Five
The Person in The System

B efore I get into this, I want to acknowledge the quote above. It is the most eloquent description I've ever seen of how to live an integrative life, full of meaning. Hold the intent constant and make up everything else, the means of accomplishing it, in accordance with your circumstances. The only trick is, be sure to define the outcome you really want *very clearly*. Otherwise, all the work only gets you to someplace you don't want to be.

All the components of any system, including its subsystems, exist for one reason—to enable the system to accomplish its purpose. If a company believes its purpose is "to make money", everyone it employs has his or her job primarily for that reason. But that's not all. Components, *including people*, must comply with the system's nature—"the way we do things around here"—whether it makes sense or not. Any function, any employee who won't adhere to existing forms and processes doesn't get to participate. It's that clear cut.

This requirement is as true for integrative systems as it is for normative or formative systems. The difference is that, in integrative systems, the forms and processes—"the way we do things around here"—are determined by the system's original purpose. They make sense, and can be changed when they don't.

Now, why do people group together in the first place? We form groups that evolve into systems in order to enhance human well-being. If our institutions don't do that, they have no reason to exist. If our institutions don't do that, they have no reason to exist. That's not a typographical error. I wrote it twice for emphasis. We'll see it again.

People are the energy of any human social system. In fact, the system exists only because of agreement between people. It exists because it serves their purposes more effectively than they can—or believe they can— as separate individuals.

Maslow's "Pyramid"

Let's look at Abraham Maslow's view of people. Dr. Maslow, who wrote several books, including *Motivation and Psychology*, pioneered the concept that self-actualization was the goal of a person's life, not "normality". What is "self-actualization"? It means to live as who you really are, as your authentic self. To do that, a person must operate from his or her innermost sense of self-evident truth. One of the distinctive traits Csikszentmihalyi found in creative people was their profound sense of purpose. Torrance found the same trait in creative children—a search for a sense of purpose. Authentic people have purpose. It gives their lives meaning.

I doubt people are born with a specific purpose. Rather, they explore and learn. They find a purpose—or several. They sense something that, to them, is worth doing, and do it. Their pursuits work because they are not chasing vague, amorphous, quantitative, form-based, *normative* goals such as "make money" or "gain power". Such goals provide no meaning because they have no particular nature, no specific character, no "spirit". They embody no inherent definition of what to do to accomplish them.

Take another look at Maslow's Pyramid. You'll see a spiritual-to-material continuum from the top down.

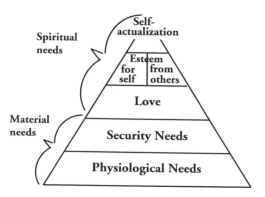

Now, let's look at Maslow's pyramid from above. And grant me just a bit of illustrative license. From this viewpoint, Maslow's pyramid is a system diagram of a human being.

I never cease to be fascinated by the way things fit together. Alone, it convinces me that reality is structured in systems. Since systems are grounded in purpose, the "random occurrence" view of reality looks at least implausible to me, if not downright silly.

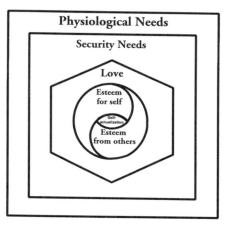

Do you remember the hierarchical relationship between systems? The larger system both defines the purpose of its components and demands that they conform to its nature. Now let's look at the interface between the person and the system in formative, normative, and integrative systems.

People in Formative Systems

A person's spiritual state and a formative system are at least somewhat compatible because people determine *what* to do in a formative system. Their job is to manifest its purpose—to create the material state that actualizes its original intent. In formative systems, people's minds acquire information, and they must know what it means. They experience the Aha! of solving problems. It's challenging. It demands creative thinking. It's the questioning, searching, experimenting, and even play that bring elements together in new and unique ways to produce the desired result. It's making up what works. This type of creative activity constantly reminds them that they exist. People in formative systems have meaning in what they do because they are creatively challenged. They know *why* they're doing what they're doing.

Creativity, purpose, meaning, spirit, origin, art, authenticity, integrity, unity, and the sense of being fully alive are inextricably linked. I throw this sentence in every so often as a reminder of what the Holy Grail is made of.

People in Normative Systems

The match for this: is this: not this:

A Normative System   **The Normative Person**   **The Whole Person**

People who are whole, or aspiring to be, are profoundly incompatible with a normative system.

Something has to give. If the individual wants to participate, he or she must "give" or, more accurately, "give up". He or she must give up pursuit of his or her spiritual self, the top three levels of Maslow's pyramid, in exchange for what is represented to be a guarantee that security and physiological needs will be met.

This graphic and the one at center above, illustrate exactly the same condition. We commonly call it "selling out". It's spiritual amputation—a psychological severing of contact with the life-force.

Corporate "downsizing" and the possible collapse of Social Security have given us ample evidence, however, that our normative systems are losing their ability to hold up their end of this bargain. Today, from any vantage point, the whole deal is starting to look pretty unappealing, isn't it?

Because control is the central theme of a normative system, it's worth a close, personal look. I usually hear the word used two ways: "We have to learn to give up our need to control" and "I want more control over my own life". At first, these statements sound paradoxical, but they're not. The "we" who have to learn to give up control are not "Me" or "Us". It's "Them"—the keepers of the norms, those with the authority to make Me and Us do meaningless, senseless things. For the person in a normative system, this is not an option. Those folks are where they are precisely because they agreed to uphold and enforce the system's norms fervently—to *make* other people conform to existing practices, policies, and procedures even when they are meaningless and senseless. "Them" are the proactive conformists—the status quo police.

"I want more control over my own life" means "I want to stop feeling compelled to do meaningless, senseless things. I hate feeling so powerless." The two statements, "They should give up control (of me)" and "I want more control over my own life", together, are a cry for freedom.

For the individual who says, "We have to learn to give up the need to control", the more accurate statement usually would be, "I have to learn to give up my need to be controlled". Does that raise a few hackles? I can hear the chorus—"We don't have any need to be controlled!"—rising up as I write this. Check that response carefully! Another way to say it is, "I have to give up my need to be told what to do!" Some people have this need a little, and some have it a lot. It's what free people are free *from*.

I believe the need to be told what to do is deeply instilled in us through the meme of "Original Sin". I was raised in the church. I heard early in life that I was a "sinner". That meant I was inherently no good, by *nature*. If I followed my authentic nature, I would go to Hell. But the church could save me. It would show me how to deny my true self. That way, I would go to Heaven. The church's message was, "Be yourself, you go to Hell. Be who we tell you to be, you go to Heaven." If I still opted to do it my way, the church responded with, "Do you really want eternal, and we mean *eternal*, damnation?" You don't have to go to church to get infected by this meme. It pervades American society. In social psychology, it's called "Theory X". Normative memes are always accompanied by some threat of dire consequences for not accepting them. That's why fear is the emotion most typically connected to them.

Do you still wonder why authentic people are so rare?

I've seen animal trainers use a technique that affects animals the same way "Original Sin" affects people. The trainer delivers severe and unanticipated punishment whenever the animal does something on its own initiative. What it does is inconsequential. That it acted of its own free will causes the punishment. After a while, most animals make the connection. They become totally dependent on the trainer to define everything they do, when they do it, and how they do it. These animals develop a very strong need to be told what to do. Without instructions, they won't *do anything*. Trainers call this "breaking the animal's spirit". It is enforced external dependency. The control memes of normative systems work the same way. They are fatal to the human spirit. Virtually everyone in a normative system is exposed. Some people have greater natural resistance than others. Most succumb. They become "the walking dead".

In normative environments, training for a life of external dependency begins at a very early age. Children are taught that "truth" comes from outside themselves. To survive, they must learn and obey. Is it any wonder that people become addicted to external substances and behaviors—drugs, cigarettes, gambling, and sex, not to mention external memes? The view has already been put forth that addictions are just compensations for spiritual amputation—loss of the authentic self. It makes perfect sense to me. It explains why drug and alcohol use have long been so prevalent among artists. Part of an artist's original authentic self is still present and operational. But that artist has also been normatively socialized. This creates an internal conflict between the authentic and inauthentic selves. Using the drug is an attempt to suppress the socialization—to put the authentic self in charge.

In *Man's Search for Meaning*, Viktor Frankl wrote:

> Just consider the mass neurotic syndrome so pervasive in the young generation: there is ample empirical evidence that the three facets of this syndrome—depression, aggression, addiction—are due to what is called in logotherapy "the existential vacuum", a feeling of emptiness and meaninglessness.

> A statistical survey recently revealed that among my European students, 25 percent showed a more-or-less marked degree of existential vacuum. Among my American students it was not 25 but 60 percent.

Why is this true? As I described earlier, the cultural foundation of the United States largely derives from Puritan Protestantism, Cartesian science, and mercantilism, which, collectively, "amounted to 'revolutionary' *intensification of normalizing* ". Progression of normalizing means that progressively greater emphasis is placed on material issues of form and process and that progressively less is placed on spiritual issues—origin, substance, purpose, and meaning. Each successive generation is subjected to greater normalizing pressure. As normative memes become more rigid and constrictive, they become more spiritually destructive. Therefore, in any aging normative system, the "younger generation", collectively, is always relatively more spiritually decimated than its parents, no matter which specific generations we're comparing. This continues until the pressure causes a bifurcation—some people continue to become more oppressed, while others break out to create new realities.

Both my personal experience and everything I've read on the subject have convinced me that children come into this world as open, integrative systems. The processes of raising children (the relationship between the child and his or her parents) and "socialization" (the relationship between the child and social institutions outside the home) boil down to processes of converting them into closed, normative systems. This is the root cause of lack of meaning in people's lives. I believe Christ recognized this when he said: "Suffer little children, and forbid them not, to come unto me: for of such is the kingdom of Heaven" (Matthew 19:14) and "Except ye be converted, and become as little children, ye shall not enter into the kingdom of Heaven" (Matthew 18:3).

When the progression of normalizing is undisturbed, as it has been in the U.S., the only clue we have that "something is missing" is the feeling of emptiness. Because we haven't understood complex systems, we haven't known what that feeling really means. It usually isn't strong enough to convince us to break with the norms to search for what's missing. But when we endure intense physical, intellectual, and emotional suffering, as many people in Europe have, we get hard evidence that "the system" can't hold up its end of the bargain. That breaks the "contract" we made to deny our spiritual selves in order to promote our material well-being. Suffering sets us free to search for the spiritual state of existence we've been denied. This is why you'll hear those who know say "embrace your suffering". In the United States, this is the up-side of downsizing. Loyal employees, playing by the rules, suddenly found themselves without the material rewards promised. The shock that accompanied this experience was their cell door opening.

Consider this: America's drug problem and the increase in both suicide and violent crime among children and teenagers are naturally occurring results of a rigidly normalized society. Conforming to rules that promote only material well-being *demands* meaninglessness. It *causes* "the existential vacuum"—psychic entropy, existential dread, emptiness, boredom, nihilism—whatever you want to call the viewpoint that life is meaningless.

Thoroughly normal people don't have internal conflict because they have completely given themselves over to being externally defined. Their fight is over. That's where the expression "the walking dead" comes from.

People who see themselves as having power often believe they are fully alive. Maybe. Maybe not. It depends on where the power comes from. There are two kinds—position power and personal power. Position power is autocratic power. It comes from being rewarded for willingness to abide by the directives of those "in authority". The further up a hierarchy, the more position power a person has. Position power is the structural mechanism by which normative social institutions perpetuate themselves. It is granted by the currently most powerful keepers of a system's norms to their most loyal followers—the future keepers of its norms. In companies, the CEO has the most position power. In monarchies, it's the king. In the Roman Catholic church, it's the pope. Position power is externally derived.

Personal power is exactly what it sounds like. It comes from within. It's a person allowing his or her authentic self to define his or her life. The highest level is self-actualization. Personal power is creative power. A person achieves it by listening to his or her instincts and by *seeing* how things work. It comes from asking "Why?" until you find the answer that fits. It's not only the ability, but the courage to recognize Aha!s, Eureka!s, and epiphanies.

The heads of normative systems give position power in exchange for personal power. They require people to sublimate personal power in order to be granted position power. This is substituting extrinsic motivation for intrinsic motivation, the development of external dependence in place of internal dependence.

Some people believe they can have both types of power. They are, for example, obedient vassals at work. But off the job, they do what they want to do. There's a fatal flaw in this approach. Alternating between authenticity and inauthenticity creates so much cognitive dissonance that internal chaos soon reigns. This compartmentalization leads to the development of different personalities. The more each develops, the greater the internal separation and fragmentation. The person becomes progressively less integrated. This is the progression of normalizing in the individual person.

Consider the following descriptions:

> Things just happen to me now, and I have no control over them. Things are coming in too fast. I lose my grip of it all and get lost.

> The picture is a stark one of impoverished imagination and frozen creativity—amazing inflexibility, banality, blocking, and clinging to the safe and obvious.

The first, from Csikszentmihalyi's *Creativity*, is schizophrenics describing their own lives. The second is Torrance's description of the results of tests for creativity given to seventy-one schizophrenics.

In describing schizophrenics, Csikszentmihalyi and Torrance are also describing a normative system in an advanced state of decline. Webster's dictionary defines schizophrenia as "a major mental disorder of unknown cause typically characterized by a separation between the thought processes and emotions, a fragmentation of the personality."

Now let's consider the "Information Age". It's about moving more data, faster. Does the term *information overload* ring a bell? Do you see any substantive difference in the basic *nature* of information overload and schizophrenia? When purpose and meaning are forbidden territory, information overwhelms because the person has no basis for organizing it and understanding what it means. It's just "noise".

A Normative System

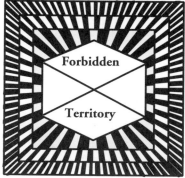

I once heard Peter Drucker say that while American companies are boasting about great advances in mechanical productivity, they can't make the same claims about knowledge workers because "Knowledge workers don't know what to do." Now we know why. Most of our knowledge workers work in normative systems. They only understand form and process, not meaning and substance. Without grasping what information means, they can't possibly know what to do. The way we're going, it's entirely conceivable that the Information Age will make schizophrenia the normal mental condition. Or perhaps we are already schizophrenic and just don't know it.

Contrast "meaninglessness, mental and physical entropy, schizophrenia, information overload, external dependency, broken spirit, and a void of creativity and life-force" to "creativity, purpose, meaning, spirit, origin, art, authenticity, integrity, unity, and the sense of being fully alive". The former is what normative systems enforce on the people who participate in them. The latter is what we want.

Overlaying Rogers' work on Land's lifecycle of systems gives us a view of the type of people who populate a system at different stages of its lifecycle, because systems demand compatibility with their nature—"the way we do things around here". When a normative system reaches its greatest apparent strength in terms of number of participants, it's populated by "true believers". It is now highly capable of causing severe "psychic entropy". It has achieved incomprehensible complexity. Its nonsense quotient is high. If it's a corporation, Chapter 11, or some equivalent, is approaching.

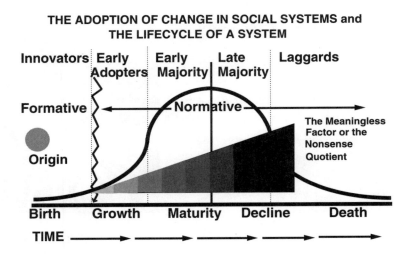

THE ADOPTION OF CHANGE IN SOCIAL SYSTEMS and THE LIFECYCLE OF A SYSTEM

Csikszentmihalyi wrote In *Flow*,

> Each social system can be evaluated in terms of how much psychic entropy it causes, measuring that disorder not with reference to the ideal order of one or another belief system, but with reference to the goals of the members of that society.

Driving the life out of its people by breaking their spirits, the organization itself becomes lifeless—a "walking dead" organization. Then we call it a bureaucracy. How do trees die? From the inside out. People and organizations die the same way.

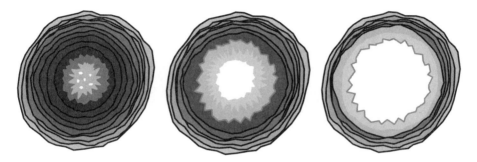

Sometimes a person imagines that he or she does not have to give up his or her spiritual self and attempts to actualize it in a normative system. This person thinks creatively, originally. He or she recognizes when things don't make sense, when they have no meaning, when they don't work nearly as well as they could—and talks about it. Those who maintain the status quo label these people heretics and exile them. Someone once said, "We have always treated our artists very shabbily". Albert Einstein said, "Great spirits have always encountered violent opposition from mediocre minds." They were both talking about the way creative people are treated by the keepers of the status quo.

This is the core irony of normative systems. By late maturity, they are literally disintegrating. Creative people have the ability to see relationships and make connections, at intangible, spiritual levels. They can put invisible things together. This is precisely what these systems need to resuscitate themselves. But the cardinal rule of the gatekeepers is to destroy deviation and diversity, which is to destroy creativity. The status quo police reject precisely what they need to survive and the creative person's ability to connect creates his or her separation. How's that for a pair of Catch-22s?

When normative systems abound, a person's quest for authenticity and meaning typically begins with separation and exile. There is no compromise. Joseph Campbell wrote *The Hero with a Thousand Faces* to describe this condition. Here's an excerpt that begins with the culture's view of the individual:

> In his life-form the individual is necessarily only a fraction and distortion of the total image of man. He is limited either as male or female; at any given period of his life he is again limited as child, youth, mature adult, or ancient; furthermore, in his life-role he is necessarily specialized as craftsman, tradesman, servant, or thief, priest, leader, wife, nun, or harlot; he cannot be all. Hence, the totality—the fullness of man—is not in the separate member, but in the body of the society as a whole; the individual can only be an organ....
>
> If he presumes to cut himself off, either in deed or thought and feeling, he only breaks connection with the source of his existence....
>
> Social duties continue the lesson of the [initiation] festival into normal, everyday existence, and the individual is validated still. Conversely, indifference, revolt—or exile—break the vitalizing connectives. From the standpoint of the social unit, the broken-off individual is simply nothing—waste....
>
> But there is another way—in diametric opposition to that of social duty and the popular cult. From the standpoint of the way of duty, anyone in exile from the community is a nothing. From the other point of view, however, this exile is the first step of the quest. Each carries within himself the all; therefore it may be sought and discovered within. The differentiations of sex, age and occupation are not essential to our character, but a mere costume which we wear for a time on the stage of the world. The image of man within is not to be confounded with the garments....
>
> For the mythological hero is the champion not of things become but of things becoming; the dragon to be slain by him is precisely the monster of the status quo: Holdfast, the keeper of the past. From obscurity the hero emerges, but the enemy is great and conspicuous in the seat of power; he is enemy, dragon, tyrant, because he turns to his own advantage the authority of his position.

A person has three choices. One is to give himself or herself over to the system's norms and join the walking dead. A second is to live with the constant internal struggle between authentic and inauthentic self. The third is to live as his or her fully authentic self. Here's Campbell's view of the third alternative:

> The essence of oneself and the essence of the world: these two are one....The aim is not to see, [although that is a prerequisite step] but to realize that one is, that essence; then one is free to wander as that essence in the world.

Isn't this precisely what we mean—and *everything* we mean—by personal authenticity, integrity, and freedom? The free person is not an isolated outcast. He or she is integrated *both* internally *and* externally.

Earlier in this chapter I wrote, "Now, why do people group together in the first place? We form groups that evolve into systems in order to enhance human well-being. If our institutions don't do that, they have no reason to exist. If our institutions don't do that, they have no reason to exist. That's not a typographical error. I wrote it twice for emphasis."

Social systems, at least in the Western world, have greatly advanced mankind's material state at the expense of our spiritual state. If their original purpose was to provide symbiotic environments for whole people, they aren't achieving it. If it wasn't, their original purpose was inadequate. Either way, we have plenty of reason to redesign these institutions. If, by forcing people to abandon their spiritual selves, the systems destroy people's quality of life and themselves in the process, there's even more reason to redesign them. *There is no natural conflict between the best interests of the individual and the best interests of the society.* That was the founding premise of the United States' form of government—an *open* system. Dualistic, normative systems created that illusion through the concept of Original Sin (Theory X). We have both spiritual and material reasons to move forward into integrative systems. Such systems keep themselves vital by enlisting and supporting vitally alive people.

People in Integrative Systems

Integrative systems resolve conflicts and eliminate Catch-22s. Rather than being self-contradictory, they are self-affirming. They transcend duality into unity. First of all, they recognize and unite the two principal complements of the system by establishing a mutually beneficial purpose. Sec-

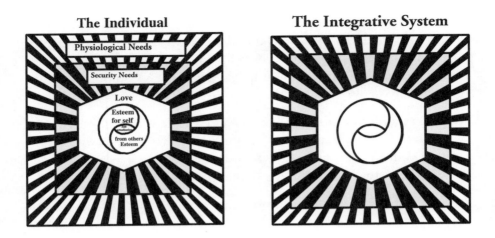

The Individual

Physiological Needs

Security Needs

Love

Esteem for self

from others Esteem

The Integrative System

ond, they unite the spiritual and material states of systems. That resolves the conflict between a person's spiritual well-being and his or her material well-being. Even though integrative systems continue to develop and become more complex, they stay rooted in their original purpose. Their complexity is comprehensible. People find meaning in them.

Converting a normative system into an integrative system follows a simple principle that breaks the cardinal rule of a normative system: return to the origin of the system, and resolve the antagonistic separation between its two principal complements by finding a purpose that is beneficial to both.

In visual terms, we go from this: to this:

This is *peaceful revolution*, not more thesis-antithesis antagonism. It's synthesis. It transcends duality into unity. It requires internally dependent people who have the courage to ask "Why?" until they get the answers that create the Aha!s that divulge meaning.

To convert a rigid, normative social institution into a fluid, integrative social system, you have to discover its origin. There may not be anybody around who can tell you about it. Even recorded history usually deals only with effects, not causes. But you can figure them out, if you can think creatively.

Once you've found a system's original intent—the fundamental connection between its two principal complements—you've found its purpose. Next, answer the question, "If this system were true to its original purpose, how would it look and how would it work, today?" Typically, what you envision will look very different from what exists. That's when you have to reinvent the system for yourself, so it makes sense. We'll go through this process, applied to the institution of "business", step by step, in Part III—Changing the System.

Only people can change social institutions. Large ones, such as "Business" or "Education," change one unit at a time. In business, one unit is one business proposition, not one company. Companies change by having a stable of integrative, open, adaptive businesses. Industries change when their members are integrative companies. Eventually, the institution changes. Changing education means one school at a time. Changing a religion means one church at a time. It all hinges on the courage of people to become open, integrative systems themselves.

Summary

The source of difficulty people in the U.S. have finding meaning is the same in all societies, the same obstacle that has plagued mankind since the beginning of civilization: normative systems. We can't find meaning because we are taught to confine our view of life to its material state—forms and processes, rules and regulations—the system's norms. People in normative systems are conditioned only to "do", according to the system's norms, without *seeing* what they're doing. This comes from purely sequential mental processing, which is often called linear, left-brain, or "Cartesian" thinking. It prevents us from thinking creatively and seeing meaning.

To find meaning, we have to be able to see things in context—specifically in the context of the systems in which they participate. To do that, we have to mentally recreate our systems as integrative rather than normative ones, beginning with ourselves. That process begins by defining our own intent for our lives. Then, most of us will have to reclaim our ability to think creatively, to be able to synthesize bits and pieces into wholes. To do that, we'll have to unlearn all the sanctions against doing it that we've acquired simply by living within normative systems. The key to it all is how we use our minds.

...ve your why? for life, then you can get along with ...y how?

—Friedrich Nietzsche, *Twilight of the Idols*

Chapter Six
Mind over Matter

Finding meaning is the ability to transcend the material, the effects, to see the purpose behind them, the cause of those effects. In normative cultures, externally dependent people look to their environment to provide what they want. They tend to believe "If only I were *in* an open, adaptive, integrative system, I'd find meaning in my life." That's not it. It is, "If only *I were* an open, adaptive, integrative system, I'd find meaning in my life." Being an open, adaptive, integrative person is, literally, a matter of how we use our brains.

The exclusive practice of linear, Cartesian thinking prevents us from seeing meaning. If we only think analytically, if we only use our quantitative, mechanical, sequential thinking processes, there's no meaning for us, no matter where we are. Our "synthetical" (a word used to avoid confusion with the common meaning of "synthetic"—i.e., not real) brain capabilities—that little-understood function that assembles pieces into pictures that produce Aha!s—must be fully operational. The principle is easy to illustrate.

We'll use a very concrete, complex system—a dog. To begin, we'll take the traditional normative, Cartesian approach. We'll measure and analyze its component parts.

COMPONENT		FORMS AND PROCESSES TO BE EVALUATED
Eyes		Overall size; weight; corneal integrity; retinal integrity; visual acuity—near objects, far objects, mid-range objects; presence of diseases—retinal degeneration, opacity/cataracts; etc.
Skull and brain		Overall size; weight; shape; bone density; bone integrity; size of brain cavity; brain size; brain weight; intelligence level, functionality of brain lobes.
Ears	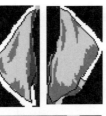	Size; type (hanging or erect); hearing range—frequency; hearing sensitivity—sound volume; presence of disease or infections.
Nose		Size; color; sensitivity—by type of odor and odor intensity; range—by type of odor and odor intensity; ability to locate source of odor; ability to discriminate odors.
Jaws and teeth		Size of jaws; compression power; number of teeth; tooth integrity; gum integrity; presence of disease.
Chest, heart, lungs, circulatory system		Size; shape; rib structure; rib integrity; lung capacity; blood pressure; heart rate; blood flow; oxygen-carrying capacity; presence of disease or toxicity.
Paws		Number of toes; number of pads; distance between pads; condition of pads; integrity of toenails; length of toenails; degree of webbing between pads.

Legs	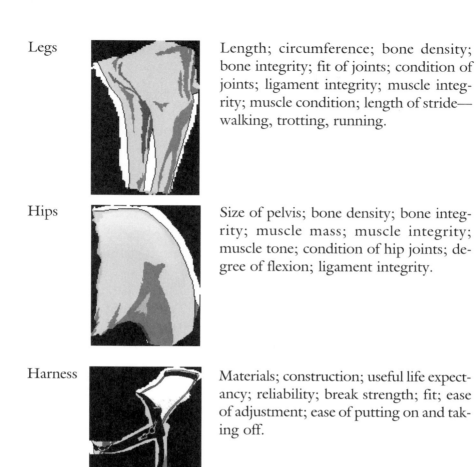	Length; circumference; bone density; bone integrity; fit of joints; condition of joints; ligament integrity; muscle integrity; muscle condition; length of stride—walking, trotting, running.
Hips		Size of pelvis; bone density; bone integrity; muscle mass; muscle integrity; muscle tone; condition of hip joints; degree of flexion; ligament integrity.
Harness		Materials; construction; useful life expectancy; reliability; break strength; fit; ease of adjustment; ease of putting on and taking off.

In addition to these subsystems of the complex system "dog," there are its digestive system, its endocrine system, its skin and hair.

Now, imagine that you generated all this information about these subsystems of the complex system "dog." You'd have pages and pages of numbers representing weights, volumes, lengths and distances, frequencies, and other measures. You'd have graphs that compare this dog's performance on sight, smell, speed, hearing, digestive efficiency, endocrine balance, muscle tone, muscle mass, bone density, and joint integrity to standards. So what? What does it all *mean?*

Look at all this information. Which is critically important? Which is important but secondary? Which is unimportant? Is any of it irrelevant? Does every piece of information look as important—or unimportant—as every other piece?

Have you ever heard the expression "God is in the details"? I've invariably heard it from people trapped in effects. They value all data equally because they have no reference of purpose to tell them what's important and what's trivial. This is what purely left-brain, linear, analytical, quantitative, Cartesian thinking produces. It's why knowledge workers have data, but not knowledge.

Now let's put all the pieces of this dog together.

It's not a generic dog, it's a guide dog. "Guide dog" is the system those components comprise. Compensating for a person's loss of sight is its purpose. The dog wearing the rigid harness is the means of accomplishing that purpose. Now look at all the data you generated. Which is critical? Which is important but secondary? Which is relatively unimportant? Which is irrelevant?

Within the context of the system "Guide dog," the data has meaning because you can relate it to the dog's ability to accomplish its purpose. Some capabilities have greater effect than others. With this frame of reference, you also realize there are critical components a purely physical analysis never considers: the dog's temperament, the person's temperament, and the compatibility between the two.

Now change the purpose of the system. Let's say the dog was not a guide dog but a racing greyhound. That changes the *meaning* of the data.

The material issues we analyze and quantify are the physical manifestations of systems. Understanding their meaning requires seeing the intent of the system they represent. Here's an example that's less concrete. It's more typical of situations we face every day.

Margaret Thorpe, who both edited and contributed to this book, has a "day job"—new business development consulting. She had guided one of her clients to a successful licensing of his creation—a collectibles ensemble. She'd identified the company most likely to buy it and why. She'd shown him what the product's unique value was to that company. She'd identified *the* most appropriate positioning for it—how to illustrate the product's distinct value to that company. And it all worked. Her client made some serious money using his creativity and being smart enough to appreciate hers.

One day, he showed up with a friend. "My buddy John has invented a product I think might have great potential for the warehousing industry," he announced, "but we want you to check it out." "O.K.," Margaret responded, "tell me all about you and it." John told this story:

"I've been working on stage sets for thirty years. Road shows come to town for about ten days. Every one has a different set, of course. And every set is made up of unique pieces. And we have to change sets between scenes. One time I was working *Phantom of the Opera*. During one scene change, we had to bring in a piano. There's a table hanging down from the ceiling from the previous scene. We have to squeeze through a narrow corridor created by two scenery panels. None of the dollies we have would work. Power equipment is too big and clumsy to use on a stage. "We've got to improvise a way to do everything on the spot. We don't have appropriate equipment and, many times, just using bodies won't work because of the weight and space limitations. I've been fighting this problem for years.

"I needed something that was small, so it would fit through narrow spaces and still provide the mechanical advantage to move heavy objects, like that piano. I also needed something I could pull instead of push, so I could always see where I was going. Here's what I designed."

John brought in a small inverted cantilever on wheels that gave a single person the mechanical advantage to be able to lift and pull objects weighing up to 1500 pounds. It could accommodate objects of virtually any shape or size. It solved his problem.

Based on what you, the reader, knows from this description, does this product have "great potential for the warehousing industry"?

Here's Margaret's answer. "It's not for warehouses," she said. How did she know?

While John was describing "the problem" this product solved, Margaret was creating a movie in her mind. She saw the stagehands moving pieces of the set around. She recognized that every time a piece was brought onto the stage, or moved, or set in place, the physical configuration changed. Every time a stage crew set a new scene, they had to figure out how to do it, on the spot. By the time a crew had placed a given set enough times to know how to do it most efficiently, the show's run was over. Then the crew got an entirely new challenge.

After she created this movie, Margaret pulled up another one on her mental screen, about moving things in a warehouse. An efficient warehouse is designed for a particular type of inventory. Its configuration changes very little. The warehouse crew moves the same type of inventory, the same way, by the same routes, using the same equipment, day after day, year in and year out.

The warehouse is highly standardized repetition—normative. The stage is continuous customization—formative. The only characteristic common to both is that people are moving things. The product was created to meet the needs of continuous customization. That's why it's not appropriate to warehouses.

Margaret's ability to recognize that the product is not for warehouses is a perfect example of how synthetical right-brain skills work. She had to collect the pieces of the situation linearly because that's how John had to communicate them. Then she pulled them together into a *picture* of the whole system—a moving picture of constantly changing conditions. By contrasting this image to that of the highly standardized routine in a warehouse, she literally *saw*, on the screen in her mind, that the wheeled cantilever's ability to fit one situation meant that it was not appropriate to the other. It solved a problem warehouses didn't have. Trade shows, live theater and music stages, film sets, and other entertainment venues do have this problem. Those are the potential markets for this device.

The pictures didn't measure and quantify effects. They displayed the *qualitative nature*, the causative dynamics of each situation.

We sometimes call this ability "systems thinking" because it visualizes a whole system. However, "systems thinking", in our highly normative society, is practically an oxymoron. Most of us consider "thinking" a *process*, not a picture. When we "think", we put ourselves into a linear, left-brain mode, which prevents us from assembling those pieces. How many times have you heard about discoveries and insights—Aha!s and Eureka!s—just "showing up" when the person was *not* thinking about the issue—in the shower, sleeping, doing something completely unrelated? That's because the person allowed the subject to move out of linear processing and into the synthetical mode that put the pieces together. This is the brain function we must "allow", if you will, in order to find meaning. It's what E. Paul Torrance called "creative thinking." Margaret Thorpe calls it "systems seeing".

The Mental Ability to Find Meaning

The process of finding meaning exactly parallels the creative or problem-solving process. It's initiated because a person develops interest in some subject, some problem, some riddle. Then the person:

1. Collects information about the subject and the problem—he or she studies it;

2. Permits a complete mental picture of the subject and the problem within it to form in his or her mind;

3. Finds, in that picture, the root cause of the problem. This is the moment of illumination—the Aha! in creativity and problem-solving. It's when people find out what things *mean*.

Different parts of the brain contribute different critical elements of revelation. This is easily illustrated by using a four-quadrant model of the brain that accounts for its functions. First, we'll look at the general model of brain function.

Type of Thinking by Area of the Brain

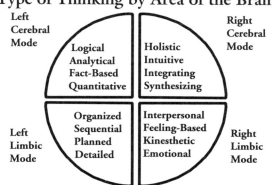

From *The Ned Herrmann Group*

Now, we place the steps of the process for finding meaning in the appropriate brain quadrants.

Type of Thinking by Area of the Brain

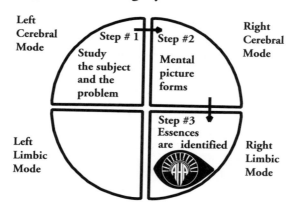

Becoming aware of, and interested in a subject, undoubtedly uses both left and right brain functions. Getting from studying the subject to understanding its essence is our concern, because people who think only linearly can't do it.

I suspect that the right limbic quadrant is the "mind's eye"—the site of Aha!s—because of the energy surge, the emotional rush that's typically connected with these experiences.

The left hemisphere is the *HOW* brain. The right hemisphere is the *WHY* brain. Normative systems train us to use our brains like this.

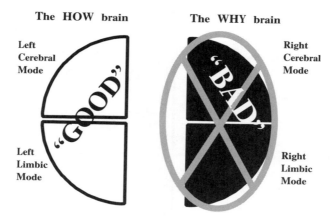

How can we find meaning in anything if we don't use the part of our brain that sees WHY?

This condition causes the viewpoint that *substantive* change is "bad". Substantive change begins with a new design. Its forms and processes aren't precisely or completely defined. People who use only their left-brain capabilities aren't sure what to do or how to do it, and they can't figure it out. They feel confused, immobilized. That's why change is "bad".

Recognizing the influence of normative systems on brain function raises an interesting question: Do those who uphold the norms, even in the face of compelling evidence to change, do so because:

a. they so deeply fear negative consequences and/or loss of position power or because

b. their minds are literally unable to comprehend anything fundamentally different since the right hemisphere of their brain has been out of service for so long?

Here's a corollary view. In discussions of creativity and innovation, two frequently used terms are "divergent" and "convergent" thinking. Personal growth, the creative process, learning, the development of new paradigms, are often illustrated as a diamond-shaped process consisting of these two major phases. This is just a different way of describing the same brain functioning that reveals meaning. "Divergence" means studying the subject, collecting new information about it, preparing to see it differently. It's left-hemisphere activity. "Convergence" means synthesizing all the information, new and old, into a new, integrated view of the subject—a new reality. It's right-hemisphere activity. Putting that new view into action is largely left-hemisphere activity.

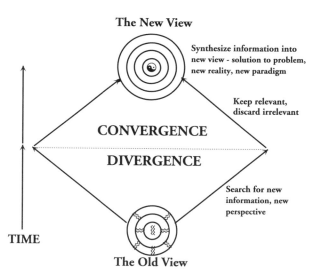

The New View

Synthesize information into new view - solution to problem, new reality, new paradigm

Keep relevant, discard irrelevant

CONVERGENCE

DIVERGENCE

Search for new information, new perspective

TIME

The Old View

The current emphasis of "creativity" seems to be on divergence—"getting out of the box". As this is primarily left-hemisphere work, normative thinkers can do it. And it is an appropriate first step. But that's all it is. Without the ability to synthesize that information into new, working systems, all a person gets is more information overload—more fragmented, more confused. Eventually, divergence only leads to an increased level of schizophrenia in "normal" people.

Summary

The spiritual and material states of systems correspond directly to the functions of the right and left hemispheres of the brain. Normal people, loyal to the status quo, predominantly use only their left hemisphere. That prevents the deviance and diversity that threatens the norms. It also prevents having the ability to find meaning. People who use their right hemisphere are the "creatives" who are often labeled "crazy". "Crazy" sometimes means "I can't comprehend what you're saying". More often, it's simply an expression of the fear of negative consequences: "You broke the rules. You'll get punished. You're crazy to take that risk." I've noticed that the "crazies" are invariably the only people around who know what's actually going on. They can see beyond the details, the tangible effects, to their intangible causes. That puts them much *more* in touch with the whole of reality than "normal" people.

The functions of the brain can be summarized as follows:

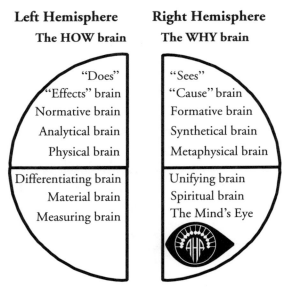

Left Hemisphere	Right Hemisphere
The HOW brain	**The WHY brain**
"Does"	"Sees"
"Effects" brain	"Cause" brain
Normative brain	Formative brain
Analytical brain	Synthetical brain
Physical brain	Metaphysical brain
Differentiating brain	Unifying brain
Material brain	Spiritual brain
Measuring brain	The Mind's Eye

Can the basis of finding meaning be any clearer? Use right-hemisphere skills to see, and we can. Stay within the confines of normal, left-hemisphere processing, and we can't. Using both hemispheres, a person can perceive both the spiritual and material states of every system in his or her life. Then, the person can find the meaning of these systems.

The ability to perceive, to comprehend, and to find meaning is exactly the same as the ability to create. To simply have the mental ability to *see* meaning, we have to retain or reclaim our creativity. Now you know why "being normal" and finding meaning in life are mutually exclusive.

Part III

Changing the System

In *Breakpoint and Beyond*, George Land and Beth Jarman wrote that mankind is at Breakpoint No. 2 in the history of civilization—the transformation from normative to integrative social systems. I agree. We're seeing a bifurcation, a split in the nature of social reality. Some people, clearly a minority at this stage, are moving on to an integrative existence. They have found, and will continue to find, meaning in their lives. Others will continue as normal Cartesian thinkers, confined to form, process, quantification—and the absence of meaning.

The next four chapters are about moving on to the integrative: changing systems by *seeing* them differently. Many of the examples cited come from business simply because it's been a major source of my experience. However, the principles apply to all human social systems, from uniquely personal ones such as marriage, a job, or raising children, to the large, formal institutions—education, government, law, health care, and religion.

For What Purpose?
(Why?)

*[Four 11]'s not cool, it's just frigging useful. Period. End of
story. God bless it.*

—Jeff Mallett, Chief Operating Officer,
Yahoo. Quoted in the *Wall Street Journal*.

Chapter Seven
The Spirit of the System

The origin of any system is the unification of its two principal complements through a common purpose. That purpose is the system's spirit. It is the system's core *"why?"*. Finding it is the starting point for re-inventing any system, from a social institution to a personal relationship.

At the core of every system is a transaction between its principal complements. In a monetary system of business, for example, it's the exchange of a good or service for money. In a barter system, it's the exchange of goods or services. In education, it's the transfer of information from teacher to student—or the development of the student's thinking abilities through exercises the teacher provides. In parenting, and all interpersonal relationships, it's the exchange of thoughts, feelings, and actions between people.

In order to find the spirit of the transaction, the critical question is, "For what *purpose* (why) does the transaction occur?" This is the essential reason the system exists. *Everything else in the system is defined by the answer to this question.*

Figuring out the two principal complements is pretty straightforward. In personal relationships, it's the two people. In education, it's the provider of the information and those who use it. Typically, that's the teacher and the students. In business, the two principal complements are the producer of the product or service and its user. In organized religion, it's the source of theological doctrine and the receivers of that doctrine. Typically, that's "the church" and its parishioners.

An *originating* purpose must meet one very strict qualification. It must be equally beneficial to *both* principal complements. That's easy to see in natural systems. The following illustration shows seven component subsystems of an ecological system: a grain plant, deer, wildfowl, soil, air, rainfall, and sun. Of course there are many more, but to include them would make illustrating the point unnecessarily complicated. We need only to consider any two to find what we're looking for. Let's take the grain plant and the deer.

The plant produces grain and oxygen. They serve as:

1. the source of its next generation;

2. food needed by the deer;

3. oxygen needed by the deer.

In return, the deer provides the grain plant with some of what it needs to prosper—carbon dioxide and organic nutrients. The deer utilizes the oxygen given off by the plant in its respiratory system and the grain in its nutritional system. The plant metabolizes the carbon dioxide exhaled by the deer and the organic nutrients from the deer's droppings. In biological terms, this is a symbiotic relationship—a relationship of mutual advantage—an *interdependent* relationship. Each principal complement utilizes the output of the other to promote its own well-being.

The cause of these exchanges is mutual benefit! And what determines mutual benefit? Usefulness! Anything that is beneficial is useful. Anything that isn't useful can't be beneficial. These are exchanges of usefulness for mutual benefit. Therefore, *the originating, unifying purpose of any system is to cause mutually beneficial exchanges of use-fulness.*

Usefulness is whatever promotes the user's well-being. It can be physical, intellectual, emotional—spiritual or material. The function of *usefulness* is not confined to any particular form.

Ignoring the user's well-being is the primary reason closed, normative systems die. When the people who administer systems—educators, managers, elected officials—focus exclusively on forms and processes, they are unaware of why those forms and processes exist in the first place. They don't know that the original intent was to produce output useful to somebody else. In traditional education, teachers teach what the educational system tells them to teach, whether it's in the student's best interests or not. Priests,

A Closed Social System

ministers, and rabbis preach the doctrine their religious denomination tells them to preach. Parishioners can take it or leave it—but they'd better take it if they know what's good for them. People in normative companies develop and maintain products and services with no concern about their usefulness to their users. Democrats and Republicans try to wrest control of government from each other while ignoring the citizens' best interests.

The spirit of the United States government, its original source of power, was that it consciously recognized the other principal complement—its citizens. Remember "a government of the people, by the people and for the people"? That's a *deliberately*, consciously, open perspective. The U.S. government has been progressively normalizing over the past two centuries, but it may be reaching the end of that rope. I believe Bill Clinton beat George Bush in 1992 primarily because of "It's the economy, stupid". That mantra had more impact than just acknowledging the U.S. citizen's material well-being. It stood for a return to recognizing the citizens themselves. It provided a stark contrast to George Bush, who epitomized the isolated, normative view. He often sounded as if he wasn't sure what planet he was on, let alone what concerned the citizens.

Perhaps a clearer, more dramatic example was the election of Jesse Ventura as governor of Minnesota in 1998. He came from "nowhere" to beat the candidates of both major parties. It was a case of an integrative candidate defeating two normative candidates. Margaret Thorpe captured the essence of the Democrats' attitude toward citizens: "We shall do to the people what's good for the people whether the people want it done to them or not." Skip Humphrey, their gubernatorial candidate, epitomized this condescension. The Republicans live by the golden rule of economics: he who has the gold, rules. They're mercantile autocrats. Compare those attitudes to Ventura's.

When asked what he'd do if elected, Ventura said, "I'll do whatever is best for Minnesota's people, and I'll be against whatever isn't." That's a statement of principle, not process. Alone, it could be interpreted as an empty generalization, but it was just one piece of the picture. After his statewide "stump", which deliberately concentrated on independent and disenchanted voters, Ventura repeated, several times, the story of the young man who said to him, "You are us". Ventura saw this as particularly noteworthy because he was focused on the integration of those who govern with those who are governed. If you listened carefully, behind Ventura's words was Abraham Lincoln's music—"of the people, by the people and for the people"—recognition of the need to benefit the other principal complement of the system.

Physics defines entropy as "the loss of energy available to do work". Apply that to systems. What's "work"? It's exchange of usefulness. Therefore, loss of exchange of usefulness is entropy, which causes death. That's even true of a chemical reaction. The reacting atomic elements exchange electrons to form the molecules of the new chemical compound. When that exchange stops, the reaction has reached maximum entropy. It becomes inert—"dead". Ceasing the exchange of usefulness is the cause of social revolt, the reason kids quit school, failed businesses and failed interpersonal relationships. Let's look at usefulness more closely.

What Is "Usefulness"?

Usefulness is *anything* that promotes the user's well-being—physically, psychologically, emotionally, aesthetically, spiritually. It can be material or spiritual in nature. Its meaning is often misinterpreted by normative systems. Take business, for example.

Usefulness is NOT simply "mechanical utility", much less what engineers typically mean by the term. They dream up product features without really considering how the product will be used. The typical engineer's definition of usefulness holds up the Swiss Army knife as an ideal: "How many features can we jam into this thing?" What he means is, "We don't know what's relevant, so let's stick everything we can think of on this thing. What the users really want will be there someplace." That's a presumption of mechanical utility not founded in reality. Maybe users can find some actual utility, if they're willing to wade through all the irrelevance. But whatever is irrelevant also *decreases* usefulness. Besides that, it sends the message, "I don't know and I don't care about you. You barely exist. But I have to do something, so here's something."

Think about gift-giving. What's the difference between a "good gift" and a "bad gift"? A "good gift" is one that supports the receiver's sense of being alive. A "bad gift" is one that doesn't. Ignoring for a moment that the specifics of this example are largely socially conditioned, why are tools "good gifts" for many men? On the surface they look like "work". But many men's reason for being is to make things or fix things. Tools support that. Many women, on the other hand, don't have that view of their reason for being. Housework is just work, not a means of self-actualization. A washing machine does nothing to support her sense of being alive.

The chances of exchanging usefulness decrease as understanding of the other principal complement and the originating purpose of the system decrease. Paul Simon's song *"Kodachrome"* described this condition in education:

When I think back
On all the crap I learned in high school
It's a wonder
I can think at all

Here's a classic example of how it works in business. And this was one of the very few new products that, by chance, survived.

The general manager of 3M's Occupational Health and Safety Products Division once asked me to conduct a broad-scale study. The flagship of his product line was disposable face masks. The two questions he wanted answered were: "Why was this product successful?" and "Will it continue?"

"If you didn't know how and why it would work, how did you get into this business?" I asked. Here's what he told me:

"Once upon a time there were two R&D scientists experimenting with a technology to mold paper into various shapes and have it stay that way. Once they got it to work, they asked each other, 'Now, what can we do with this?' One suggested paper dresses. 'Nah!' said the other, 'That's been done.' But, being on the subject of women, he added, 'But what about paper bras? A woman could wear the bra for a few days and throw it away. She'd never have to wash it.' That was their idea of the product's unique reason for being."

[Here we are, one paragraph into the story, and we've got two male "teckies," enamored with their new technology, deciding it should be useful to women for breast support. This might look like recognition of the other principal complement, the user, but obviously it's not. Just how much do you think these two actually knew about how women view this subject?]

"Each asked his wife what she thought. Being supportive, loyal wives, they answered, 'Oh honey, you're so smart. What a great idea!' They just didn't mention they wouldn't wear one on a bet. Having completed their market research, the two convinced management to build a pilot plant. It consisted of die-cutting machines stamping out everything from 32As to 44DDs.

"They named the product, packaged it, and gave it to the sales force that called on department stores. These guys usually called on the stationery buyer about tape and such. They made a detour to see the lingerie buyer, who, of course, was a woman.

"The roars of laughter that erupted from lingerie buyers' offices caused the sales guys to slink out without bothering to open the door. With bright red faces, they called headquarters: 'Did you clowns ever check this out? That was the worst experience of my life!

"The home office cheered! One possible application of the technology had been eliminated. They were one step closer to finding a home for it."

[This is the trial-and-error approach of which Richard Dawkins said, "The trouble with overt trial is that it takes time and energy. The trouble with overt error is that it is often fatal."]

"'O.K., the bra idea didn't work. Now we've got all these die-cut machines. What can we do with them?' someone asked.

"'Well, if we cut the bras in half and add rubber bands, we'll have face masks,' someone offered.

"That's what they did. Industry bought 'em like crazy. That's how we got into this business.

"The thing is," the general manager continued, "We don't know *why* industry bought 'em like crazy—or if they're gonna keep buying 'em like crazy."

What I found out was that while Tweedledum and Tweedledee were playing with the bras that became face masks, the Occupational Safety and Health Administration (OSHA) changed its primary focus from accident prevention to air quality. Manufacturing plants found themselves equipping workers with canister masks. Canister masks are heavy. They restrict breathing, induce fatigue, and interfere with vision. Morale and productivity plummeted. Adding insult to injury, plants had to sterilize the masks every night, further increasing costs.

Into this situation blindly stumbled a product that was lightweight, induced far less fatigue, and interfered less with vision. It was also disposable, which eliminated the cost of sterilization. It provided a way for companies to comply with OSHA's regulations without destroying their profit. That's dramatically superior usefulness. No wonder industry bought 'em like crazy.

The company had provided dramatically superior usefulness—without consciously intending to do it, knowing how to do it, or knowing that it had done it. This was one of that tiny percentage of systems, closed at birth, that survive by chance. Without the knowledge provided by the study, the company would never have known *why* it was successful. Nor would it have known to update its definition of usefulness, as conditions in the use system changed, in order to perpetuate its success.

The exchange of usefulness makes systems work. It is the integrating, unifying spirit of *all systems*—between two people or between thousands or even millions of them. When people say, "I want to make a difference," they're saying, "I want to be useful, because that's how I know I'm really alive." In personal relationships that work, each partner champions the other's whole existence—especially the things that make the other feel alive. This causes marriages to prosper. Its absence causes divorce. Parents who champion their children's natural, authentic existence typically have strong, lasting relationships with them. Parents who treat their kids as faults to be corrected have kids who break away from them eventually.

What is "love" if it isn't championing another's whole, authentic existence? To know how to do that, however, requires championing your own whole, authentic existence.

The exchange of usefulness creates the bond between the principal complements. It is reciprocal. The more one member provides what the other utilizes, the stronger the bond—the more symbiotic they become. This is true for man-made and natural systems. In business, the more useful the product, the more the user will pay to have it. Providing relatively less or no usefulness breaks the bond—both ways. If the deer can no longer utilize the grain, what does it do? It goes elsewhere and finds another food source. Its droppings and CO_2 are no longer available to the grain plant. When one partner stops championing the other, it may or may not injure the other. *It always injures itself.*

Those who swear to uphold a normative system's forms and processes are the primary cause of its downfall. Because they ignore the system's origin, they ignore the other principal complement and the purpose that was mutually beneficial. They *don't* champion *the other*. Take American business. About 99 out of 100 people would say that the purpose of business is "to make money." That can't *possibly* be the original purpose of business. Why not? Because it considers only the producer's well-being, not the user's. It's not *mutually beneficial*. It's not a *unifying* purpose. While it isn't the originating cause of business, it is the cause of business failures.

Where did this definition come from? Mercantilism. And what were mercantilism, Puritan Protestantism, and Cartesian science? They were *"revolutionary intensification of normalizing"*. "To make money" (accumulate wealth) became the purpose of American business via capitalism, the [economic] "American Dream". Our forefathers took a highly normalized system, saw only the effect beneficial to themselves, and called it the purpose of the system. Wrong! Dead wrong! They never asked themselves, "What is the *essential* purpose, the originating cause of business?" The effect of this particular mis-definition shows up most dramatically just where you'd expect, in the creation of new businesses. They have at least a 95 percent mortality rate. Management can never get to the root cause of failed and failing businesses because they don't know the original intent of business itself.

In *The Structure of Scientific Revolutions*, Thomas Kuhn pointed out that innovation almost always comes from outside the established system. Now you know why. The maintainers of the established system don't know its true purpose. They have no basis for redesigning its operations to continue achieving that purpose. They can't even see that operations need to be redesigned.

The relationship between the normative definition of the purpose of business—"to make money" and the original purpose of business—to exchange usefulness—is this: *providing greater usefulness* than users can get from other providers is the *root cause* of the *effect*—"making money." Money is simply a promissory note of usefulness that the producer receives in exchange for usefulness provided in the form of a product or service. Therefore, if a producer wants to make money, its *purpose* for any *specific* business has to be "to provide competitively superior usefulness." That's "championing the other" as it applies to business.

Now you know what those Catch-22 accounts of business insanity in Chapter One were really about. They were accounts of normative minds reacting to an integrative view of their own situation—minds trapped in effects, blind to cause.

Usefulness and Creativity

Championing another can be the consummate creative challenge, especially in interpersonal relationships, when both people are pursuing self-actualization. These are conditions of perpetual personal growth by both principals. He and she are likely to be different today than they were yester-day or last week. This is the zenith of "making it up as you go along". It's fun. But since any "rule" might be appropriate for no more than a few days, rules don't work. Forms and processes change constantly.

The critical skill is the ability to think creatively, to think—are you ready?—transcendentally. That's not mystical. It doesn't require strange exercises and rituals. Little children do it—until it's taught out of them. All creative thinkers do it. It's what gets them exiled as heretics.

Go back to the word pairs in Chapter Three, where we substituted "both - and" for "either-or". That's the beginning of *transcendent thinking*. It simply means to see beyond the appearance of separation and antago-nism into the reality of complement and unity. Joseph Campbell de-scribed it in *The Power of Myth*:

> It's a matter of planes of consciousness. It doesn't have anything to do with what's happened. There is a plane of consciousness where you can identify yourself with that which transcends pairs of opposites.

This is not new stuff—or New Age stuff. It's very old stuff. Twenty-five hundred years ago, Lao Tzu wrote:

> And opposites get their meaning from each other and find their completion only through the other....

> When opposites supplement each other everything is harmoni-ous. Without compulsion, each supports the other....

> Profound intelligence is that penetrating and pervading power to restore all things to their original harmony.

Transcendent thinking is profound intelligence; it is the essence of creativ-ity. We know it as Aha! or Eureka! the moment when all the pieces of the puzzle fall into place and reveal not only the whole picture but also *"why"*—its *meaning*. A person doesn't have to be Joseph Campbell or Lao Tzu to do it. Before civilization and the rise of normative systems, our ancestors did it as a matter of course. Consider this account from an unknown anthropolo-gist about a story carved on the walls of a cave.

It seems a certain clan became very skilled at killing mastodons. They knew how to chip stone to produce sharp edges for piercing tough hide. They understood momentum. They mounted heavy stones on long wood handles for impact. They were great trackers. They'd learned that circling a mastodon confused it. While it was trying to figure out what to do, it was an easy target. This was all great, except the clan got sick and tired of mastodon meat.

One day, the mastodon masters came across a neighboring clan. This bunch didn't know squat about killing mastodons, but it knew a lot about fruits and berries. It had learned how to weave grass baskets to carry and store them. It had learned, the hard way, which tasted good, which tasted bad, which were poisonous. Picking fruits and berries wasn't as thrilling as killing mastodons, but the food supply had a lot more variety.

"Whoa! This is great," observed one of the mastodon hunters, "Fruits and berries. Just what we need to cure our mastodon-meat monotony. Let's kill 'em and take their stuff."

"Hold on there a second, Swifty," responded the chief. "They know fruits and berries. We don't. If we kill 'em, we'll get a few and that'll be it. We'll be right back where we started. Look, we never eat all the mastodon before it rots, anyway. What say we trade some of our mastodon meat for some of their berries? We can keep that up for a long time and we'll all be better off."

"But when do we get to kill 'em?" asked Swifty.

"We don't, stupid. We want them to live and prosper because that's how we get a steady supply of fruits and berries—provided they like mastodon meat, of course. This is called enlightened self-interest. You better take notes."

So the mastodon hunters traded meat for fruits and berries, and both clans lived happily ever after—well, within the limits imposed by saber-toothed tigers and the like. The chief was a transcendent thinker. He understood exchange of usefulness for mutual benefit. But remember, this was well before the rise of civilization.

In religious and spiritual pursuits, concern for "the other" is often called "a life of service". Unfortunately, it is always presented within the context of normative systems, so it has an "either-or" character: "Don't be selfish, don't think about yourself, just care for others". That's a dualistic view. It's the "caretaker's creed". It has three fatal flaws. First, it puts caretakers in the position of deciding what's good for others without understanding those others. That's not mutuality. It denigrates, belittles, and patronizes the others rather than championing them (see Democratic Party). Second, the normative view of "selfish" and "unselfish" is devisive— "either-or". An integrative view of championing the other's existence is *both* consummately unselfish and consummately selfish. Remember, "When one partner stops championing the other, it may or may not injure the other. *It always injures itself.*" Honestly championing the other is the most effective way to guarantee your own well-being. Third, if the caretaker cares for others without reciprocity, he or she commits at least emotional suicide. In addiction and abuse rehabilitation, unreciprocated caretaking is called "enabling". Enablers fall into black holes of entropy that drain all feeling of being alive. This condition is by no means confined to those who live with addicts and abusers. Anyone who chooses to "work inside the comfort zone" of a system that abuses him or her is an "enabler". These people perpetuate what they *don't* want. That's a core Catch 22 that prevents them from finding meaning in life.

The Potentially Fatal Flaw in Changing the System

To transform any system, new or established, from closed, normative to open, integrative, we have to identify its principal complements and the mutually beneficial purpose that unites them. Then we have to redesign the system so it faithfully actualizes its intent. Then, to realize meaning from that system, we have to implement that design, that is, think and act according to it. Here's what we're doing: We're uniting two complex systems, let's say a man and a woman, or a producer and users, to create a third complex system beneficial to both—a marriage or a business.

Many of us can identify what we want from the other, in our job, our marriage, our relationship with our kids, our kid's education, our education, our worship, in the products and services we buy. Being the *user* is relatively easy. But what about being the *producer*? We know what's useful to us. But what's useful to the *other*? The only way we can answer that question is to *know* the other. We're not only woefully unprepared for such a task, we've actually been trained *not to do it*. Unlearning that training, and then learning how to know others, is the greatest obstacle I see in our efforts to move on to integrative systems.

The "battle of the sexes" provides an example of how difficult it is. Men and women go through life armed with disparaging images of each other that masquerade as understanding—"men are ... women are ... " Where did these fallacious images come from? They're more of the normative memes that parasitize our minds. But the clincher is that many members of both sexes actually adopt the characteristics of their normative image, making the memes self-fulfilling "truth". Now imagine what it's like to unlearn all the false truths you hold about being a member of your own gender as well as the opposite sex, especially when both of you act them out as if they *were* true. It may help to remember that the "battle of the sexes" is not fought by men and women. It's fought by organic he-bots and she-bots. Opening up to your "feminine side" or "masculine side" may be horribly normative language, but it works. It just means casting off the constraints of normatively defined gender roles to embrace your whole, natural self. It's amazing how that increases your ability to know someone else—of the same or of the opposite gender.

Moving on to integrative systems requires us to throw away what we think we know and *start from scratch*. We can only know ourselves or another as a *system*—with my, his, or her own purpose and means of accomplishing it. If we can't literally *discover*, free of what we think we already know, we can never actually *know* ourselves or others. Without that knowledge, we can't be relevant. We can't provide usefulness. We can't know *what to do, for ourselves or anyone else*. That's the potentially fatal flaw in attempting to go from normative to integrative systems. It's the reason the next chapter exists. Consider the following as warm-up exercises for it.

1. You are a parishioner. You go to your appropriate place of worship on the appropriate days. For what purpose? Does the experience help you achieve your purpose? What parts do? What parts don't? Does any part of the experience actively thwart achieving your purpose?

    Now, change roles. You're the priest, the minister, the rabbi, the doctrine provider. What is your goal? What is the church's goal? What are your parishioner's goals? Are they essentially the same, that is, unifying? Look at the church's tools—its building, its artifacts, its events, its services. Do they help you achieve your goal?—the church's goal?—the parishioner's goals? Which do? Which don't? Which thwart parishioners' abilities to achieve their goals? Does your place of worship champion your parishioners, *according to their definition*? Do you have any idea even how to think about answering these questions?

2. Consider your child's education. What is the educational system's purpose? What does the kid want to get from his or her education? What do you want the kid to get from it? Do you, the kid, and the educational system have a common, unifying purpose? How do the educational system's tools—its curriculum, its teaching methods—contribute to accomplishing its goal—to accomplishing your kid's goal—to accomplishing your goal? How does the education he or she is receiving enhance his or her life? How does it diminish his or her life?

3. What's your purpose as a parent? What does your kid want? What will best prepare your child for his or her adult life? Does your child agree with that? While we're on the subject, what's your goal for your own life? How does it affect your goal for your child? How does it affect your child's goal for him or herself? What does championing your child's life mean to you? What does it mean to him or her?

These are tough questions. If finding meaning in life were easy, we wouldn't have been agonizing over it for the past several millennia. At this point, we're about as ready as we can be to pursue that lost art which determines the amount of meaning we find in our lives—knowing *the other*.

But how does one search, not for new answers, but for new questions? Looked at in a new way, our familiar world can all of a sudden reveal new meaning.

—Lee Smolin, *The Life of the Cosmos*

Chapter Eight
"Grok"-ing the Other

This chapter brings together everything from the preceding seven. It's about the perceptual skills necessary to transcend our separation from *the other* at the core of any system we're in. This is the essential ability we need to be integrative ourselves and to create integrative systems. We need it to be able to "grok" the meaning of the things of life.

For his novel *Stranger in a Strange Land*, the science fiction writer Robert Heinlein invented the word *grok* to mean deep, complete comprehension. Here's how two characters in his book describe it:

> "It was necessary to go beyond shape to essence in order to grok."

> "Grok literally means 'to drink' but this means to understand something so thoroughly that you merge with it and it merges with you. Then, and only then, can you love something, fear something, hate something. Anything you hate, you also, by necessity, love. Grok means to understand so thoroughly that the observer becomes a part of the process being observed—to merge, to blend, to intermarry, to lose personal identity in group experience."

To find meaning in our lives, we have to be able to "grok" what's going on, both inside and outside ourselves.

This chapter uses two examples to illustrate "grok"-ing—comprehending "the other" and, from that, the foundation of mutual benefit. These examples are ordinary and commonplace. Why? Because that's where we live most of our lives. We consider the ordinary and the commonplace boring because it has no meaning to us. It doesn't lack meaning. We just don't see the meaning. We don't because all we see are its forms and processes. When we can see the ordinary and commonplace as systems, we can see meanings. Then, it isn't boring. Things aren't boring. The normative view of them is boring.

Most of us have seen examples of people "grok"-ing each other at extraordinarily complete, even synchronized levels—people who can start and finish each other's sentences, who approach telepathic communication. They *know* each other. They understand each other's values and, if they're really in touch, each other's dreams. They have a systems grasp of each other. But if you asked one to paint his or her picture of the other, he or she probably couldn't do it because these images are held in the subconscious. We want to make this ability conscious.

Here's a focal point that may simplify this daunting task. Recognize that everything we do can be viewed as providing the other with a tool of some kind, in the broadest sense of the word. It may be a physical, mental, emotional, aesthetic or spiritual tool. Whatever it is, it helps that person get where he or she wants to go.

Books are a scholar's tools. When Mom and Dad want a break from cooking and still have to feed the kids, a fast-food restaurant is a tool for achieving that goal. When a person buys insurance, he is buying a tool to prevent financial disaster. I once heard a woman who sold women's fashions say, "Women use fashion to appear to be whom they'd like to be." So, don't think of tools only as mechanical utility. Remember Peter Revson's remark, "We don't sell cosmetics, we sell hope."

Now, think about primitive man, the original toolmaker. His goal was to survive. He had to eat and defend himself against being eaten. As the user of a tool, he knew what best served his purpose—what was most useful to him. As producer, that's what he made. For him, this was easy. The same individual was both user and producer. Use told him what to produce. Although we've lost sight of it, this principle hasn't changed.

This is the level of "knowing the other" that's necessary in order to be *useful*. It's the ability to make another's reality your own. That's "grok"-ing. To do it, you have to be a seer. But nearly anyone *can* be a seer.

The Seer

Whether a person is trying to understand a problem or create a solution, "grok" another person or a social institution, the personal skills required are the same. Architects, artists, and designers are more likely to be *seers* than people in other professions.

They've managed to retain their synthetical, right-hemisphere, creative-thinking skills *and* have found supportive environments. But they're not the only ones. I've met market researchers, library managers, information systems people, R&D scientists, engineers, ministers, organization and human resources development people, business managers, machinists, sales people, and even a couple of marketing people who are seers. They retained this ability *in spite of* their cultural environment.

A *seer* could also be called a sympath. An archetype is the character Counselor Deanna Troi of *Star Trek: The Next Generation*. She's called an *empath*, but that's a misnomer. Empathy is "the projection of one's own personality into the personality of another in order to understand that person better." That's not what we're talking about. The common meaning of "sympathy" is "pity." That's not it, either. A little-used definition of sympathy is "an entering into, or the ability to enter into, another person's mental state, feelings, emotions, etc." That's it: that's the ability to "grok".

The most complete and effective *seers*:

1. Can both *see* and *do*. They are "whole-brained". They are as adept at identifying a problem at its essential cause as they are at solving it. In fact, their ability to identify problems at this level often makes the solutions self-evident;

2. Instantly integrate content and process. They know *why* they want information and, therefore, what information they need. They keep track of the information they need to get, and the information they've already got, throughout the process of getting it. Their minds constantly shift from process to synthesis and back again;

3. Are highly impartial. They bring no agendas of their own;

4. Are highly independent. This is a prerequisite to being impartial;

5. Understand normative society. Society allows people to discuss some subjects openly but not others. The seer must know the social context of whatever subject he or she is exploring to know how to explore it;

6. Know what motivates people. This enables the seer to pick out the critical influences in the information gathered.

Seers working in any given system also need to know its original purpose and the current definition of its purpose.

The effective seer sees what the other person sees in his or her mind's eye—not directly, as in "mind reading", but indirectly, by assembling bits of information into mental pictures—the Aha! experiences. Doing this requires a person who can, on the one hand, identify and record users' mental, emotional, and physical processes, and, on the other, see the pictures this information paints. Is this a lot to ask? Within the confines of normative thinking, it's impossible. But the limitations come from normative training, not from human mental capacity.

Seers constantly *originate* images based on the information they gather. They don't recall similar pigeonholes and pick the one that looks most alike. Remember Margaret, creating a movie in her mind of erecting stage sets based on the information her client gave her? That's what seers do.

The Process for "Grok"-ing the Other

Now, let's look at the process. It's always in the context of a specific system. The first example is quite simple. It's teenage girls who figure skate. You can view this example from at least two viewpoints—as a parent trying to comprehend a child or as a skate manufacturer trying to understand its users.

Keep in mind that the following is just process description. What an investigator would actually *learn* depends on his or her ability to *see*. In a normative mindset, following the steps of a process is all that's required. Finding meaning requires grasping the *intent* of the process. Following the steps of a process is "How". Finding meaning is "Why".

The goal of this investigative process is to be able to see *the other* and the system in which he or she participates, often even more completely and fundamentally than *the other* sees it, at least on a conscious level. That might sound impossible, but remember the old saw about forests and trees? It's actually easier for a capable outsider than an insider. A person in a normative system is usually so focused on its material forms and processes that he or she is rarely aware of the dynamics behind them—consciously or subconsciously. An outsider can discover the whole system, starting with its originating cause, because he or she doesn't have all those details blocking the view.

The Design of the Process

The discovery process follows the hierarchy of systems, but it can move in either direction. The direction it takes depends on its purpose. It can go from the larger system to one of its subsystems, or it can build upward from smaller subsystems to larger systems.

Let's say a skate manufacturer wants to understand what a "better" figure skate would be. The basis for understanding that is the answer to the question "What is the purpose of the figure skate?" That answer can only be found by first understanding the purpose of the system in which it's used—figure skating. The typical normative answer to this question is "The purpose of a figure skate is to figure skate." That's based on tangible behavior. It includes only the form, not the motivation behind it. I could call it a "Skinnerian" answer. It's useless. It tells the skate manufacturer nothing about what to do to provide a better figure skate—one that provides greater *usefulness* than other skates.

A parent pursuing this investigation would have a very different purpose. Let's say he or she is trying to understand the child by understanding the child's interests. This difference in initiating purpose creates a different investigative process. For the skate manufacturer, the process would start with the relatively larger system—figure skating—and move to the smaller one—the figure skate itself. For the parent, the process also would start with figure skating. But then the parent would look at the kid's lifestyle—all her activities. By identifying the motivations behind these activities, the parent can begin to develop a picture of the whole child.

The Skate Manufacturer's Process

The Parent's Process

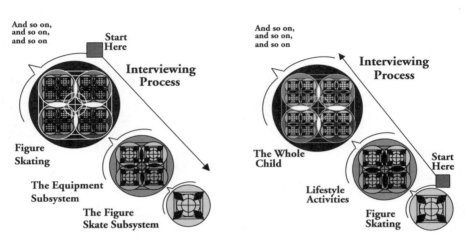

"Grok"-ing a person is typically a matter of recognizing common patterns that represent his or her essence. Take me, for example. I can, after decades, say that I am, *essentially*, a systems designer. "Systems design" is inclusive of my artistic instincts, my education in engineering, biochemistry and genetics, and my profession—new business development. It's the common thread, the dominant pattern that runs through everything I've done. It took me a long time to figure that out. I had to build up from the specifics, then step way back to look at the whole that those specifics represent. I also had to originate the label as it applied to me, since it is normally used only in computer-based information systems and software development.

In a normative society, people keep trying to pigeonhole others to create the illusion they understand them. I remember when a senior manager in one of 3M's divisions was going around asking questions about me. I paid him a visit. "I hear you're trying to find out about me," I said. "You'd probably get better information if you went directly to the source, so here I am. What do you want to know?"

"I want to know what you are," he replied. "Are you a marketing guy, a market researcher, a strategic planner, or a training and development person?" "Yes, I am," I replied. He was sorry he'd asked.

Substituting classification for understanding is the basis of stereotyping. What are stereotypes? They're memes based on superficial observation of form and process without understanding underlying substance. The reason stereotypes are so often "true" is that externally dependent people adopt those characteristics because they believe that's who they "should be". To get an accurate picture, one person must *originate* his or her image of not only who the other appears to be, but often, of the authentic person underneath the facade. One thing we can count on in normative systems: what we see is rarely what IS.

To illustrate the process, I'm going to use the approach the skate manufacturer would take rather than the parent. It's more concrete. We end up with a whole definition of a better skate. The other process ends up with a partial image of a person's nature.

We start with the system that uses the skate—figure skating. We identify its purpose. Then we identify its subsystems, the major components for achieving that goal. We define their specific goals; then, their operating processes. At every level, we find out what's working (satisfactions) and what isn't (dissatisfactions), because the goal of this process is to define a "better" figure skate. This is an investigative, learning exploration. It's a *conversation* in which the seer is genuinely interested in *the other's* viewpoint. Remember, its purpose is to find out what would champion *the other*. The seer initiates the process and then follows *the other* through each level, wherever *the other* may go, allowing *the other* to discuss what comes to mind until she exhausts her thoughts. This is how the seer gets to see that person's situation through *that person's* eyes.

This is very different from the way market researchers typically interview potential or actual users of a product or service—or the way many parents talk to their kids. Under normative rules, the interviewer goes into the interview with a set of expectations. Discussion is confined and controlled by those expectations. It's not genuine. It's more like an inquisition because the producer or the parent *assumes* a *dominant* position— me ruler, you subject. Bringing expectations to a conversation makes it a test. They imply a morality or "correctness" to *the other's* responses— which *the other* picks up on. This creates separation rather than connection. It diminishes, rather than increases, understanding because the subject becomes more concerned with figuring out what the ruler wants to hear than with how she really sees the issues being discussed.

O.K., now let's have genuine conversations with several teenage female figure skaters. We'd find two very different purposes for the same activity. One group of young women want to become competitive figure skaters. The others figure skate for recreation. These goals generate different systems for accomplishing them.

The drive to compete creates a system with five major subsystems: physical conditioning, mental conditioning, immersion, instruction, and equipment. Recreation creates a system with two major subsystems and one minor one.

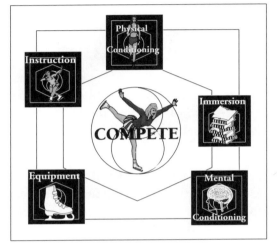

Mental conditioning covers activities such as improving focus ("Inner Golf," "Inner Tennis") and self-confidence. Immersion means activities related to competitive skating—reading magazines, attending events, and belonging to clubs.

At this point, if you're a parent, and you've just found out that your daughter wants to become a competitive skater, you now understand why she's involved in all those activities and where her attitudes about them come from. To learn more about her, the next question is, "Why does she want to become a competitive figure skater?"

If you're a skate manufacturer, the next question is, "A better skate for whom—aspiring competitors or recreational skaters?" Chances are, "better" for one is different from "better" for the other. Aspiring competitors want their skates to give them a "performance advantage"—the old "competitive edge". Recreational skaters want their skates to protect them from injury—sprained or broken ankles in particular. These injuries seriously interfere with recreating, both on and off the ice. These different meanings of "better" call for different responses—different products.

I don't want to bore you with process description, so I'm going to continue only with what "better skate" means to aspiring competitors.

This all sounds pretty commercial, but consider the process in a more personal context. Does someone in your family have a birthday coming up? What would be a *great* gift? How can you find out? What makes a great gift great? A great gift is something that helps the person receiving it accomplish a goal important to him or her. A gift is also a physical, intellectual, or emotional tool. Pick out something that person loves to do. It might be gardening, traveling, or what have you. Then follow this same process.

The seer reviews all the subsystems—mental conditioning, physical conditioning, immersion, instruction, and equipment—even though his or her specific goal is to define a more useful skate. This provides additional context that, very often, provides the *why* behind the information specific to skates. All this information is interrelated. It doesn't just answer the immediate question, "What is a better skate?" It also reveals to the seer the other's whole picture of the subject. As such, it shows how to market skates most effectively to these users and often identifies other new product opportunities. It creates the complete picture of *the other* that is the "grok". The skate manufacturer needs all this knowledge in order to know both how to create a more useful tool and how to market it effectively.

After reviewing the major subsystems, the seer and the user focus on skates, in particular. The user describes her purpose for skates. Then the seer gathers specific information about the performance characteristics and physical traits that provide that function. He or she is looking for *the user's perception of how the product's features help her accomplish her goal.*

This is a microcosmic example of how the purpose of a system defines its component parts and their relation to each other. Producers (and parents and people in general) rarely have this knowledge. Let's follow the conversation:

The skater has said she wants "skates that give me a competitive advantage". Then the seer asks, "What about the skates, themselves, is most important?" Her first response might be "fit".

Seer: "Why—what does 'fit' mean?"

Skater: "When I compete, I have to feel that the skate, the blade, really, is part of me, an extension of my foot, not an appendage. If the boots fit too tight and pinch, it hurts. I might unconsciously compensate—and bobble or fall on my landings. If the skate is loose, I can feel that, too. It's not an extension of my foot. I don't trust it. That makes me lose concentration, too."

Seer: "What else is important?"

Skater: "Support."

Seer: "Why—what does support mean?"

Skater: "It's related to fit. I want my skates to increase the strength of my ankles without restricting their movement. Sure, a splint will increase stability, but it makes my ankle immobile. To hold true lines, my ankles can't wobble, but they can't be rigid, either. Maybe it's impossible, but that's what I want."

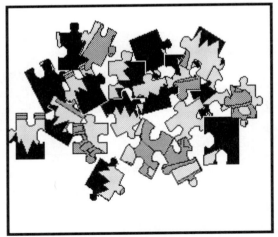

The seer asks about all other characteristics of skates, such as blades—preferred materials, their ability to hold an edge, the preferred way to attach them to boots. He or she asks about the aesthetics of boots, materials used, even the laces the skater prefers. The seer is gathering this information bit by bit, like the pieces of a jigsaw puzzle.

Synthesizing the Information

These are the Aha!s— the pictures of what the details mean that linear, normative thinking alone can't provide. After he or she has listened to several skaters, the seer must synthesize these bits and pieces of information into complete pictures. First comes the picture of the overall system and its component subsystems. Then comes the pictures of the component subsystems. Then comes the picture of the ideal product. It defines the traits the product must have to be a uniquely useful "tool" in this system.

THE IDEAL

Next, the seer must learn how well current products match this ideal. This is how he or she finds the specific opportunities to better champion *the other's* cause. For the skate manufacturer, this identifies the nature of the opportunity to provide competitively superior usefulness. The process continues:

Seer: "So, how do you feel about the skates you're using now?"

Skater: "They're really great."

Seer: "Is there or was there anything about them you didn't like?"

Skater: "Well, yes. They didn't fit right, at first. But you know, I must have strange-shaped feet. Didn't I tell you that my biggest fear with physical conditioning is that I'll blister my feet because I have such trouble finding jogging shoes that fit?"

Seer: "Yes, you did. Did the skates not fit right the same way jogging shoes don't fit right or in a different way?"

Skater: "In the same way. In fact, whenever I buy any kind of shoes, if they fit across the ball of my foot without pinching, they're loose in the heels. If they fit in the heels, they're too tight across the ball. Then my feet hurt, and I tire easily. That's the bigger problem, so I get shoes that fit across the ball of my feet and figure out how to fill up the heels to stop the slopping around."

After hearing this from several skaters, the seer has another Aha! He or she has found an important piece missing from the picture of the ideal, which defines what a "better" skate would be for many skaters with this goal. The seer has *functionally* defined a more useful tool—a skate boot that more closely conforms to women's feet. Remember—*essential* definitions of problems present self-evident solutions.

This is the basis of creating a new complex system of exchange of usefulness. Its two principal complements are the skate manufacturer and teenage girls who aspire to become competitive figure skaters. The intent that benefits *both* is "a skate that fits so well, it's an extension of her foot". The skater gets what she wants and reciprocates in kind, giving the manufacturer what it wants. This intent unifies the two.

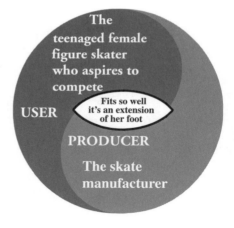

This "grok" of *the other* allows the producer to know much more than just what a better skate would be. The skate manufacturer has also learned:

1. That the dominant influence on the skater's choice of products is her instructor;

2. How skaters view competitive products—their "image" of competitive products;

3. From reviewing the immersion subsystem, what magazines these aspiring competitors read, what televised events they watch, which ones they attend;

4. From reviewing the physical-conditioning subsystem, about an additional new product opportunity—conditioning shoes (jogging shoes) for female skaters—which may have a much broader market than just figure skaters;

5. From reviewing the equipment subsystem, that aspiring figure skaters buy most of their equipment from specialty skate shops, typically located in skating rinks, not shopping malls;

6. From interviewing skaters at rinks, the environmental influences on skaters, such as the subtle brand-reinforcement devices that decorate skating rinks.

This is what a "systems view" of *the other* means—a comprehensive understanding of attitudes and behaviors *grounded in their primary cause*. In this case, the skate manufacturer not only knows what product to make, he also knows how to position it, advertise it, and distribute it. This producer now has the knowledge to be *wholly relevant* to the user. This ability to be *wholly relevant* is impossible in normative systems.

Consider how truly knowing *the other* (users) would affect people's work lives. Think about its impact on the quality of work life in the skate manufacturing company, for example. All the decisions people make, all the actions they take, are guided by this common knowledge of *the other*. Their work lives *make sense* because of it.

Imagine this condition between parents and kids and people in general—wholly relevant communications.

A More Complex System

The example of the skater is relatively simple—a simple product and a specific group of people—teenage women who want to become competitive figure skaters. The following example is entirely "commercial". It's a research study I did on the use of compressed air in auto manufacturing. It's included to show how the same process discloses the same picture, in a much broader, more complex system. This example illustrates the greater demand on a seer's ability to visualize systems as their size expands. It also exemplifies the blindness of normative systems. It shows how powerfully a system's purpose, as defined, controls its nature, whether that purpose makes sense or not. Finally, it shows how *an inaccurately defined purpose drives a system to do nonsensical things*. This is the story of an electronic controller for air compressors.

An electronics company had developed a controller to turn air compressors, used in manufacturing plants, on and off according to demand. The company's idea was that it would reduce waste. Waste is compressed air that exceeds demand and is "blown-off" into the atmosphere. The controller wasn't selling.

My initial research revealed there were two distinctly different use systems within the general area of "compressed air used in manufacturing". One was "constant demand". The textile industry typified it. Compressors were turned on, delivered a constant volume over long periods of time, and were turned off. The other use system was "variable demand". Different departments of the manufacturing plant came on-line at different times. Further, the amount of air used by any one department often changed throughout the day. Demand was highly variable hour to hour, shift to shift. Automotive manufacturing typified this situation. "Constant demand" was a simple situation with no problems. I investigated "variable demand" in automotive manufacturing.

The power plant supplies compressed air to manufacturing. Four people had major stakes in its performance: the power plant manager, the manufacturing plant manager, the plant engineer, and the corporate energy engineer. Collectively, they were the potential users of the controller. The operation of the power plant was its potential use system.

Because the power plant was a subsystem of the whole manufacturing operation, I first needed to know how the manufacturing plant manager viewed his role in achieving company goals. My first question was, "Why does your job exist?"

He replied, "The purpose of my job is to keep this operation running smoothly."

"Why?" I asked.

He said, "When we run smoothly, we make money. Delays or slow-downs reduce our output, which makes every unit cost more to produce. If our plant goes down for a day, or loses the equivalent of one day's production, that costs us $110,000. My primary job is to ensure that the company meets or exceeds its COGS (Cost of Goods Sold) expectations."

This description was on the tip of his tongue. Whether his numbers were accurate or not, I knew exactly how his priorities were structured.

The plant engineer saw things much as the plant manager did. That's why he still had his job. His primary objective was to prevent equipment breakdowns—for the same reason—to prevent downtime and reduced output. To make more money, he should improve plant efficiency (further reduce COGS), but that might require change. He only got to pursue that goal after he'd done everything possible to prevent breakdowns in the existing system.

The power plant manager's first response to, "Why does your job exist?" was "to keep the machinery running". Then I asked, "Why, what is the result of keeping all the machinery running?"

He said, "To be sure that all the compressed air manufacturing needs to do its job is available when needed [to prevent reductions in output]."

The corporate energy engineer at first said his job was "To evaluate the use of all types of energy throughout the corporation." That's a process answer.

I replied, "O.K. so you know how much, of what, is being used and where. So what?"

He responded, "Then I can identify opportunities to reduce our energy usage."

My next question was, "Is your concern with reducing energy primarily driven by recognition of a need to conserve energy or is it primarily intended to reduce the cost of energy?" (What's the *cause* of what you do?)

"Reduce the cost," he said.

These people all knew what the driving force was, even if they described it differently. Eventually everybody, in one way or another, said "to make money".

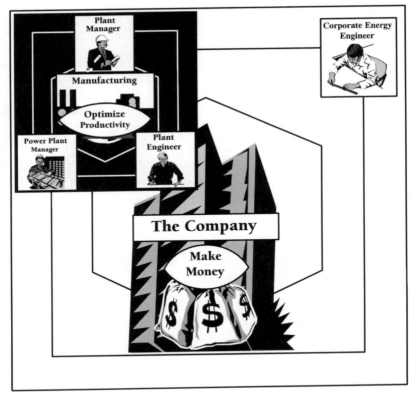

All this investigative process amounts to is constant probing for the causes behind effects, motivations behind behavior, the *why* of things.

Now I had to understand the use system itself—the process of producing compressed air as it related to their goals.

First, I toured the power plant. I observed the compressors, identified their nature, how each type—reciprocating, screw-type, and turbine—worked, their maximum output, individually and collectively, their "dwell" times going up to maximum output and coming back down to zero, and how they were coordinated to meet demand. I reviewed charts of demand by shift, by day, by week. I saw how the power plant worked. Now I needed to know what all this meant to the guy actually responsible for it, the power plant manager.

"How do you run this so that manufacturing has all the air it needs when it needs it?" I asked.

He replied, "We look at the week's production schedule. We plot how much air is going to be needed, when. Then we figure out what combination of compressors can deliver it. Different compressors have different maximum capacities. They build up to it at different speeds. We set up a schedule that shows what compressors will be on, when, and when they have to be turned on and off. Then, once we get the schedule figured out and posted, it's just a matter of turning the right compressors on at the right time."

This really *was* a complex system. Without all the context developed by touring the power plant and studying the charts, I'd never have understood what this answer meant. Now I was ready to find out if there was any opportunity to provide greater usefulness in this situation. "Are you experiencing any problems achieving the results you want?" The power plant manager gave me a four-part answer:

1. "Sometimes the plant changes its production schedule, and we have to abandon ours. Then we're scrambling to get in sync with the new schedule. If we don't make it, departments start screaming."

2. "Sometimes, after we've gone to all that work of figuring out which machines should be on and off, the guy responsible screws up. He's doing other things and forgets. Then departments are screaming."

3. "We have fifteen compressors of three different kinds to give us the production flexibility we need. Each one has a different capacity, and each type has a different dwell time. Sometimes the plant gives us a demand schedule that makes it damn near impossible to figure out what the best combination would be."

4. "To make sure that departments have all the air they need when they need it, we put in a margin for error. We blow off the excess. That costs money but it's better than having them screaming for air."

This was my first Aha! moment. These were not four different problems but two. Three statements described one problem—the inability to keep the compressed-air supply synchronized with demand. The fourth described the problem created by the current solution to the first problem. If the power plant underproduced, it caused slowdowns. That cost "lots" of money. Overproducing prevented slowdowns. It was cost, but wasting compressed air cost a lot less, overall, than underproducing. Given the intensity of the plant manager's No. 1 priority—to optimize productivity—the power plant manager *always* erred on the side of overproduction.

Assembling all this information into a picture of this system, which included its problems, produced a set of functional product requirements for an electronic-air-compressor controller that would be more useful:

Product Purpose

The purpose of this product is to synchronize compressed-air supply with compressed-air demand more reliably (in order to eliminate the cost of waste while guaranteeing adequate supply).

Operating Requirements

1. Must work with reciprocating, turbine, and screw-type compressors in combination;

2. Must be able to withstand a hostile environment—high temperature (up to 120 degrees), high humidity, and oil-polluted air;

3. Must "anticipate" increased demand to *guarantee* adequate compressed air is available when needed;

4. Failure to meet demand cannot occur more frequently than once in 1,000 requests. A request is any case of demand by any department coming on-line during any shift;

5. This .999 level of reliability must be sustained for the first four years of operation;

6. Must "anticipate" decreased demand to prevent "blow-off" and minimize energy waste. The controller must reduce "blow-off" by at least 20 percent.

These are fairly specific requirements. Here's the point! Can you see how they relate *directly* to the company's primary goal? The electronic controller is a small component of compressed-air production, which is a subsystem of manufacturing, a subsystem of the company. Yet the criteria that determine *greater usefulness* in this controller are determined by the *company's* goal—"to make money". That's how pervasively powerful the purpose of any parent system is, whether it's functional or not.

The electronics company, also a normative organization, had ignored its principal complement in this potential business system, the variable demand compressed-air producers who would use its product.

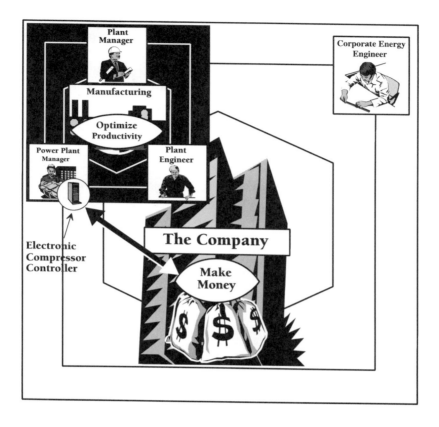

To work, any tool must fit into the system that uses it. This controller was certainly no exception. That's the source of Operating Requirements 1 and 2, working with reciprocating, turbine, and screw-type compressors in a hostile environment. Turbine compressors, alone, are dominant in the textile industry. They provide high volumes of air, efficiently, but have long dwell times. Flexibility is their weak point. They work fine in *constant-demand* manufacturing. To have the flexibility it needs, *variable-demand* manufacturing uses three types of compressors—turbine, reciprocating, and screw-type.

Here's the punch line: the electronic controller, a product intended to synchronize compressed-air supply with demand, only worked with turbine compressors. It fit the system that had no synchronization problem—and it did not fit the system that did. Most new products and services fail because they are irrelevant but just "off the mark". This product was remarkable in that it was *perfectly* irrelevant—180 degrees out of sync with the problem it was intended to solve. That may be a milestone in normative Catch-22s.

Now, think about the quality of work life in the electronics company. How much sense could things possibly make? How much accomplishment could employees feel? Contrast this culture to the skate-manufacturing company that had thoroughly "grok"-ed *the other*, knew what it was doing and why. In which of the two companies would people find more meaning, more sense, in their work lives?

Misdefining the purpose of a system—in this case, the socio-economic institution of business—leads to misdefining the purpose of its subsystems—specific businesses—and their subsystems—R&D, product development, marketing, production, sales, customer service, etcetera. It actually *drives* people to do meaningless, senseless things—the mindless decisions *Dilbert* points out so vividly. The alternative is to create organizations of people who see and operate from the system's true purpose. These are open, integrative systems that make sense. Things *work!* People find meaning in their work.

Think about it. How much sense and meaning could anyone find in a system that has the wrong idea about why it exists?

[W]e are not all alike; there are diversities of natures among us which are adapted to different occupations... as we have many wants, and many persons are needed to supply them, one takes a helper for one purpose and another for another; and when these partners and helpers are gathered together in one habitation the body of inhabitants is termed a State... And they exchange with one another, and one gives, and another receives, under the idea that the exchange will be for their good.

—Socrates, in Plato, *The Republic*

Chapter Nine
The Integrative Organization— Everybody's a Designer

I magine what it would be like if a bunch of people who all had open, integrative perspectives and different, complementary capabilities formed an organization. Since most of us have no frame of reference for such a vision, this chapter seeks to help develop one. Here I describe life in an open, adaptive, integrative organization. The example I use is a business organization. Work life in this organization is never "one year of experience twenty-five times". Every month, every week, even every day, provides new challenges.

Here's how Csikszentmihalyi described it:

The creative process starts with a sense that there is a puzzle somewhere, or a task to be accomplished. Perhaps something is not right, somewhere there is a conflict, a tension, a need to be satisfied.

Open systems actively *seek* these puzzles, these "conflicts" and "tensions". How different that is from "avoid deviance, diversity, variation, and change". This is the *essential* difference between an open, integrative, adaptive organization and a closed, normative, mechanistic one. The former lives to solve problems. The latter exists to avoid them. Embracing and solving genuine problems energizes both people and organizations. And the more fundamentally a problem is embraced and solved, the greater the energy boost. Conversely, avoiding problems just drains the energy off, creating entropy.

Integrative systems have a steady supply of puzzles and new tasks precisely because they *are* open and adaptive. People continually design and redesign what they do, and how they do it, to assure that they achieve their purpose, and the system's purpose, in the face of changing conditions. The people create their responses from *within*—from their own talents and experience. They are not mindlessly adhering to rules and regulations. Csikszentmihalyi calls this "autotelic":

> The "autotelic self" is one that easily translates potential threats into enjoyable challenges, and therefore maintains its inner harmony.... For most people, goals are shaped directly by biological needs and social conventions, and therefore their origin is outside the self. For an autotelic person, the primary goals emerge from experience evaluated in consciousness, and therefore from the self proper.

This describes the *internally* dependent, fully alive person, someone who has, as Joseph Campbell put it, *"resonance within [his or her] own innermost being and reality, so that [he or she] actually feels the rapture of being alive."* Robots and machines cannot be autotelic, by definition. Only fully alive people can. Life in an open, adaptive system not only *has* meaning; it is *defined* by meaning. Everyone must know what things *mean* in order to know what to do.

I actually experienced life in an open, adaptive business system with my new business development unit at Pillsbury. To put this unit together, I surveyed each of the skill areas I needed (research and development, market research, manufacturing, etcetera) for malcontents. Some of those doing a lot of bitching were hopelessly untalented. Others were far more talented than the organization would let them be. Those were the ones I wanted. They were easy to spot. Their bosses were only too happy to reassign them.

My management style was always criticized with some version of Theory X—"These people have to be managed. They have to be constantly watched and directed. You don't do that. You're not *managing* them." You bet! By this time I'd figured out that "management" meant process control applied to people. That's primarily what the people I wanted were bitching *about*. They wanted *authorship*—a chance to feel *they* had made something happen. My primary job was to give them that opportunity. They held purpose and results sacred, not process. All I had to do was point us in the direction we wanted to go, get the hell out of their way, and keep us synchronized. I didn't know it at the time, but this was a self-organizing, open, adaptive system. We understood our common goal. Each of us understood our contribution to achieving it. We continuously designed and redesigned our processes in order to make our contributions. Had I operated like the traditional process-fixated manager, I would have prevented us from doing our job. This was the group that developed the twenty-two new product concepts, of which twelve were viable businesses, that brought the core insanity of the system into focus and ended my career at Pillsbury.

The Structure of an Open, Adaptive Organization

An integrative organization for conducting business has the same structure as any open, adaptive system. The illustration on the next page represents a manufacturing business, but the relationships of people in any social system that desires to be open and adaptive parallel this structure. It shows the progression from *purpose* at the system's center through its materialization to the final results it produces. In the case of a business, those final results are the physical exchanges of goods or services for money. They produce satisfaction for the customer/user and income for the producer/provider. *User satisfaction* and *producer income* are the measures of *usefulness* in a business system.

The product or service—the distinctly useful tool—links producer to user. It's the "artifact of the [system's core] promise", the business organization's reason to exist. When, and *only* when, the producer knows the promise of the business can the producer know how to create and sustain an integrated system. The core promise defines what product or service to provide to which specific users. From that, the most effective communications and distribution methods can be easily identified. Communication knows what to say, to whom, via the most efficient media.

Distribution knows how to get it to them. This is *designed business*. It defines the entire system, including the results it will produce.

By simply adding the names of company functions—the groups of people who, collectively, are "the producer"—we get the appropriate structure of an open, adaptive, integrative business organization.

An Integrative Business Organization

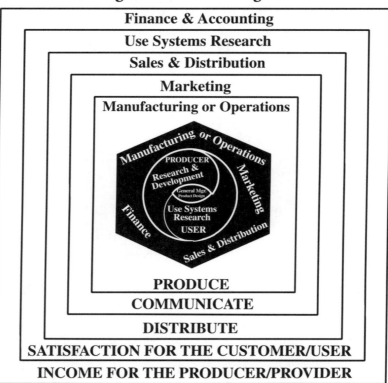

This structure isn't new. Ever since Eric Trist developed socio-technical systems in the early 1960s, organization development professionals have recognized it, or something like it. In recent years, "the learning organization", "the self-organizing system", "the horizontal organization", and "the High Performance Work Organization" have been introduced. These initiatives have had mixed success. In virtually all cases, they've met with resistance. In some cases, the people promoting them were simply fired to end the threat. Other initiatives, actually implemented, failed outright. The most successful ones improved communications and work flow. They increased *efficiency*. That was the highest achievement *possible*. They *couldn't* improve performance beyond this. Do you know why?

The practice of organization development (OD), in any environment—companies, churches, schools, government—is confined to group work processes. These normative systems don't allow *what* they do to be challenged, only how it's done. Therefore, OD practitioners are confined by the normative rules of the larger system. While their organizational model may be open, it is always subjugated to a closed, normative set of operating rules. That's why new organizational structures raise false hopes. Employees know that the things that don't work are largely due to *what* the organization does. But they want to believe a new structure will make things work a *lot* better. When things work only a little better, if at all, their hopes are dashed and the organization goes into depression. Without changing the parent system—the practice of business—itself, the *best* OD *can* do is improve efficiency. In many cases, the new structure enables the organization to do the wrong things faster and cheaper. At best, it makes negatives less negative. At worst (the other best), it allows the organization to kill itself faster.

First comes people. Individually, they become open, adaptive, integrative systems. Then comes associations of these people—open, adaptive organizations. It's all people, people. All businesses, companies, all social organizations and institutions are nothing more than agreements among people. The difference between normative and integrative organizations is simply what

A Traditional Normative Company

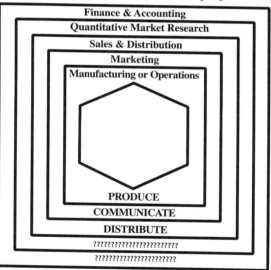

the people agree *on*. In a normative system, it's a set of rules, based on form and process, that control thoughts and actions. In an integrative organization, it's original purpose—making up whatever forms and processes are most appropriate for achieving it.

Since people power the integrative organization, let's see what their roles are, beginning with the core of the system.

How It Works

General Management and Product Design

General management and product design sit at the center of the open, adaptive business system because their primary responsibility is to integrate its two principal complements, producer and user, and *keep them integrated*. General management is the primary *integrative competency*—a true leadership function—not status quo policing. This job's purpose is to sustain the integrity of the system. The general manager is literally the supreme champion of *both* principal complements, the chief advocate of the promise that unifies them, the business's purpose. That's how he or she keeps the business, the organization, and the *people* fully alive.

Product design is one of the general manager's two chief instruments because it originally creates the uniquely useful product that manifests the business's promise and, as necessary, redesigns it to keep that promise.

The General Manager

The general manager must not only see systems, he or she also must be particularly capable of integrating the diversity in them, from the promise that unifies the two principal complements at its core to the multitude of specific tasks necessary to manifest that promise. In normative systems, those with the broadest responsibility are forever trying to prevent the boat from rocking. In integrative systems, they steer it skillfully through turbulent and uncharted waters. They are truly visionary, equally at home in spiritual and material states. They keep one eye on the system's purpose and the other on the process of achieving it.

Product Design/Research and Development

Product design is the other truly integrative competency in an open, adaptive business organization. It must know both principal comple-

ments intimately. It must unite function—what the producer can do with what is uniquely useful to the user, in a specific form—a product or service. If a product is inadequate in either *function* or *form*, the business will fail, no matter how potentially competent the balance of the system. This is the zenith of creative problem-solving.

The most talented designers I know *live* "outside the box". For them, the critical question is, "What is the purpose of what I'm trying to create?"

Designers think both conceptually and specifically. First, they create the design. Then, they integrate the properties of materials, forces, reactions, environmental, and human factors to put it into a tangible form that provides the desired function under the actual use conditions. Note that we've resolved the separation between "design" and "engineering". This process is not *either* conceptual *or* tangible, general or specific. It's *both*.

Research and development and engineering are where the company has its arsenal of technologies—its problem-solving capabilities. In an open system, the R&D people aren't caught up in "not invented here". They are aware of technologies the company has and of others it may need, to be able to develop the most useful product. They think in terms of the *function* of technologies—*what* they do—as well as how they work. They need to be close and constant colleagues with use systems research people and product designers because they must have the same intimate understanding of the problem to be solved. This relationship permits designers, R&D scientists, and engineers to create to an externally defined objective—the user's best interests.

Use Systems Research

Use systems research—"grok"-ing *the other*—is the third *core* competency required. Use systems research is *not* "market research," "quality function deployment," "customer satisfaction studies," or any of the other adventures in data collection that typify normative systems. If you're familiar

with these, you could tell from the previous chapter that "grok"-ing *the other*" is very different. It's what an organization must learn, in order to be able to learn. It generates the knowledge a producer needs to develop, market, and distribute "tools" that promote their user's best interests.

Use systems research, product design/R&D, and general management create the original spiritual state of the business and sustain its integrity. This demands broad, original, creative thinking.

Manufacturing, Marketing, Sales, and Finance

In a normative business, manufacturing, marketing, sales, and finance are strictly tactical functions, documents entitled "strategic plan" notwithstanding. In an open, adaptive business, they are both design and implementation functions. They must be able to both "see" and "do". Manufacturing, or in the case of a service business, operations, must figure out the most effective means of consistently generating the system's output. It must have the flexibility to redesign its systems whenever the product or service must be redesigned. Marketing must design the communications system that gets the most appropriate message to users, most efficiently. Sales must create, and modify when appropriate, the system that makes the product or service most available to those who will use it. Finance must understand the entire business system in order to fund and account for it in the most useful ways. To do their jobs, all these people must know the origin of their business system. It's their foundation. It's the knowledge they need to make the decisions that best accomplish the business's purpose. Because people in every function make decisions that *originate* with them, their work life is meaningful to them. It reaffirms their existence.

Now that we have some sense of the people and their relationship to one another, we can look more closely at how they actually operate. But before we get into this business example more deeply, let's step outside it to look at other social institutions. Can you see how the principles apply to religion, education, government, health care? They can just as easily use "use systems research" to understand parishioners, students, citizens, and patients. From understanding *the other*, they can create programs that champion *the other*. Health care is a prime example. How much money is wasted in health care every year because of "trial and error" diagnostic processes caused by specialists with narrow perspectives and the "least cost" progressive testing requirements of HMOs? How much could be gained if the physical and the psychological branches of health care worked together? If the patient's best interests were recognized as the core purpose of health care, accurately diagnosing health problems, *the first time*, would increase drastically. That, in turn, would make health care more affordable.

The Open, Adaptive Living Business System in Action

Let's say we've conducted use systems research. We've found a specific opportunity to provide competitively superior usefulness to a specific group of customers. Now what?

Product Design

First, the designers use the definition of superior usefulness to establish the design objective.

Let's go back to the figure skating example. The design objective would be: "a boot that readily conforms to women's feet". As people who see systems, the designers suspected they might find some clues about how to do that in sports medicine. They found that most women's shoes, including athletic shoes and skate boots, are proportioned the same as men's, just smaller. But women's feet are proportioned differently. They're wider across the ball relative to the heel. Virtually *all* women's footwear "slops" in the heel. That may be tolerable in casual footwear. In athletics, it's a fatal flaw, the antithesis of "fits so well, it feels like an extension of my foot".

(Don't you find it amazing that every time you find a very specific example of something that doesn't work, like women's footwear slopping in the heels, you can trace it back to ignoring the other principal complement of the system? That's the universal effect of dualistic normalizing.)

There are usually several ways to provide the desired *function*. In this case, one would be to build boots proportioned like women's feet. Since the manufacturer already makes women's skate boots on forms (called "lasts") that have men's proportions, this is the most costly solution and it still doesn't account for small differences between the feet of any two women who wear the same size. The designers investigate ways to optimize fit on any *one* woman's feet. One alternative is to put inflatable pockets in the sides of the boot around the heel. Another is to use one of several conformable materials, inserted into the boot, followed by the skater's foot. The material conforms to both contours. These are different *forms* that provide the same *function*. These last two more completely achieve the goal—"fits so well, it feels like an extension of my foot".

Throughout the design process, *function* is the primary language. Unlike "specifications", it's *qualitative*. It's not only the common language between producer and user (ministers and parishioners, teachers and students, doctors and patients) it's the language that unifies all elements of the producer or provider organization. *Form* only has meaning *in the context of function*. For the skate boot, its specific materials, the means of joining them, shapes and sizes are only meaningful in so far as they accomplish "fits so well it feels like an extension of my foot".

Competition

An open system views the concept of "competition" *very differently* than does a closed system. Remember, a closed system ignores the other principal complement and the intent that unifies the two. Therefore, it can only define competitors as those who do the same thing it does. "Direct competitors" are those who do the same thing almost exactly the same way. "Indirect competitors" are those who do the same thing a slightly different way. Companies focus on other companies that provide the same products. The Democrats focus on the Republicans and vice versa. Religious denominations decry each other. I remember a minister telling his Missouri Synod Lutheran congregation, "The Jews, of course, are lost. So are the Catholics. The Baptists, Methodists, Presbyterians, and Congregationalists don't get it, and frankly, I'm not very confident of the American Lutherans, either. This is the place to be if you want to get to Heaven."

In an open system, competition is *anything* that provides *usefulness* to the same system of use. For a business, it's any product or service that provides the same function under the same conditions. Closed, normative organizations are typically blind to competition that provides superior usefulness in a very different form. This is *why*, as Thomas Kuhn pointed out in *The Structure of Scientific Revolutions*, "Innovation almost always comes from outside the institution." Here are a couple of examples.

One day I was talking with the business manager of 3M's Rescue™ scouring pads. At the time, it was a light green, soap-filled, synthetic sponge laminated to a dark green, non-woven abrasive pad. It was for scrubbing pots and pans. The business manager was looking for ways to increase sales. I recommended that we first determine how consumers perceived the product relative to its closest competitors.

"What do you mean relative to our closest competitors?" he asked. "We don't have any!!!"

I asked him, "What do you think Brillo™, S.O.S.™, Chore Boy™, Chore Girl™, etcetera are?"

"They're not competitors," he responded. "They use metal mesh or metal fibers. We use non-woven fabric. Besides, they don't have a sponge." This was beyond simple form-fixation. This brand manager was in perceptual solitary confinement on the subject of competition. This next example is a bit more subtle.

The Ultra-Tech Electronics Company has just perfected the proverbial "better mousetrap". It uses high-frequency squeals of joy, undetectable to human ears, to invite mice in. There's no food, no frustration with mice that steal bait and run. The owner never needs to bait the trap. When they pass through the trap's portal, mice are instantly, mercifully, and quietly electrocuted. That eliminates the annoying "snap". The mouse goes to a cremation chamber. Emptying the trap is like emptying an ashtray. No more, "Eeuug! You pick it up and take it out, Harry." No blood-stained traps to clean. And the ashes can go in the compost pile because there's no organic matter, just mineral remains. Technologically and ecologically—except for the mouse's demise—this is clearly "the mousetrap of the twenty-first century". Anyone who considers themselves at all contemporary couldn't live without it, right? And management feels the price is very reasonable, considering it's a complete home mouse-processing facility—$89.95 retail.

The idea of literally having the proverbial "better mousetrap" has management ecstatic. Even the word "better" sounds inappropriate. It implies some relevant point of comparison, which management doesn't see. They're fond of saying, "We have no competition." That's why they gleefully, yet conservatively, predict that 65 percent of all U.S. households will buy it. "Who could live without it?" they tell their stockholders. At a manufacturer's selling price of $44.50/unit, this is a nifty $3 billion business over the next ten years or so. It has a gross profit margin of 70 percent. The $100 million the company invested to develop it makes this look like the highest return-on-investment opportunity in history.

Management may have overestimated the product's potential just a tad. First, homes that don't have mice are not in the market. Second, homeowners who don't mind baiting and emptying traps are well satisfied with their 99¢ solution. They're not in the market, either. Third, there's a powerful competitor management has overlooked. It's also silent. It never needs to be emptied because it's self-cleaning. It uses no electricity. It's available everywhere, often doesn't cost a dime, reproduces itself, and doesn't have to wait for mice to come to it. It goes to them. It even comes in a wide variety of decorator colors.

Competition is first based on *functional usefulness*, then on *form*. The more similar the form, the more obvious the competitor—and the less potential for meaningful superiority in usefulness. The form fixation of normative systems generates undifferentiated, commoditized, *meaning-less* products and services. This is true for all social institutions. Consider what's happening to some of our largest ones.

Politics

"Washington," said Dan Rather, "couldn't be more surprised if Fidel Castro came loping through on a hippopotamus." While shocked pundits ask, "How did Jesse Ventura do it?" it might be better to ask what the *people* did.

Both political science and business textbooks tell us that the way to get majority or market share is to define our target market(s) and then craft the message that will most appeal to them. It doesn't matter much if the message is true or not; the important thing is that it's what we think "they" want to hear.

Both liberals and conservatives believe it. It's the old Theory X view of people—not too smart, simple, slothful, selfish, greedy, sinful, and in desperate need of management by the better and brighter. A bunch of Minnesotans, however, said, "He's the only guy who acknowledges our existence."

Health Care

Politicians rail against HMOs. Managed-care plans try to corral physicians. Employers wrestle benefit plans. Legislators mandate more coverage for more conditions. And people? What are they doing? Walking around the whole mess and spending more and more of their own money for "alternative medicine". Visits to alternative practitioners have increased 47 percent since 1990, according to the *Journal of the American Medical Association*. People may have spent as much as $34.4 billion out of their own pockets in 1997 for alternative care.

Business

So many jobs are so stressful. The alternative practitioners offer stress relief. Organizational developers hatch plans for more humane corporations. Human resources people hand out advice on balancing family and work. What are people doing? Saying, "No, thanks" and going to work for themselves—as free agents, as entrepreneurs.

Now, back to the open, adaptive business organization.

Manufacturing/Operations

Open, adaptive systems don't cause much change in the nature of manufacturing from the way we know it today. The primary effect is that products designed to be uniquely useful to specific groups of users typically have smaller volumes than commodities. Therefore, manufacturing must increase its flexibility to be able to produce a wider variety of products in smaller volumes and to accommodate the redesign necessary to sustain a product's competitively superior usefulness. "Agile manufacturing" becomes a major asset.

Open, integrative business systems affects service businesses and the customer service function of product businesses more profoundly because these are direct interfaces between a representative of the producer and the user. Here, companies reach the zenith of "niche" or "target" marketing—*markets of one. Day in and day out, the people meeting the users, one-on-one, have the greatest influence on whether or not the producer keeps its promise*. Each customer is a *unique other*. Rules don't work—only principles apply. The front-line people have to customize, on the spot, to create the best fit with each customer. This is continuous "instant design". Their skill at it determines the strength of the bond between producer and user.

Now consider the view of front-line people held by traditional, hierarchical autocrats—in any institution. They are "underlings", relatively insignificant subordinates. But they are also the people who do or do not manifest the core promise. Take a long look at wait people, store clerks, flight attendants, technical support, and field-service people from this point of view. Now you know what a *horizontal* perspective looks like. Notice where you're looking. You're not looking *down*. You're looking *outward*—to where the real action is.

Front-line people champion *the other* when they know it's in their best interests. When the organization tells them to protect the company *against the other*—dualistic antagonism—that's what they do—and break the bond in the process. Therefore, the job of those behind the front line is to integrate the best interests of its front-line people with the best interests of *the other*. This is about 180 degrees from the way it works now.

Giving people individual determination not only allows them to do their job, it also makes their jobs interesting and challenging. It puts meaning in their work lives. Their energy level stays up because they know that what they do definitely makes a difference. When they're equipped, it makes a large, positive difference. When they're not, it makes a large negative difference.

My oldest daughter got her degree from Penn State in restaurant management. There, she learned its *mechanics*. She also worked as a waitress, hostess, and assistant manager in several restaurants. There, she learned the *purpose* of the business. She preferred being a waitress. That was the only place she could experience the *spirit* of the transaction. To her, every customer was a distinct partner. Her ability to champion the customer was immediately reciprocated in her tips. She actually developed a "practice"—a loyal clientele that moved with her, from restaurant to restaurant. Do you think the restaurants wanted her? The independents did. But when she left a corporate restaurant chain, her comment was, "These people have no clue about what makes this business work, and they don't want one. Clueless and proud of it."

Marketing

In normative companies, sales pushes what the company makes via direct personal contact. Marketing pushes what the company makes via indirect, impersonal contact (advertising and promotion). In open, adaptive businesses, marketing and sales are both design and implementation functions. They create systems faithful to accomplishing the purpose of the business itself.

Marketing communicates, in the most effective, efficient manner, the product or service's superior usefulness—its ability to help the user accomplish his or her purpose. It speaks in the users' language. It employs the same forms as before—packaging, advertising, and publicity—but as a complete, integrated communications system. This requires design skills. It requires full understanding of the use system, the users and the product's unique usefulness to them. Here's a good example of how the origin of a business system is also the foundation of its marketing subsystem.

Several years ago, I helped create a line of instructional fishing videos for a client. First came the use systems research. I found out why people go fishing. There are three reasons: to get away from work or home; to increase sense of self; and to strengthen family ties. I named them, respectively, "Escapists", "Students", and "Family Man"—which includes women.

"Family Men" were the least dedicated to fishing per se. It was just one of several parent-child bonding activities. This type rarely watched fishing shows, bought or rented fishing videos, or read fishing magazines. They were not potential users of fishing videos.

Both Escapists and Students, however, were acting on feelings that they didn't really exist in the normative systems surrounding them. The Escapists simply wanted to escape. They watched fishing shows, read fishing magazines, and bought or rented fishing videos in order to emotionally transport themselves out of the daily grind. They wanted lots of action—"white water". It engaged their attention and made the escape more complete. They hated instructional videos. Those were more of the linear, analytical directives they were trying to get away from. Overall, they were pretty satisfied with most of the fishing videos already available.

The Students also felt invisible. Their goal was to find something that gave them a sense of being—greater autonomy—where the outcome depended on their individual ability to produce it. They'd chosen fishing. They researched it. They attended lectures, watched instructional shows, and gathered all the data they could. They learned about different species of fish, in different locations, in different seasons, water clarity, water temperature, pH, edges, structure, bodies of water, lines, rods, reels, lure types, colors, fish senses, cold fronts, and warm fronts. They were very dissatisfied, not with fishing videos per se, but with the lack of results they were getting from all this work. Most suffered *extreme* information overload. All this data wadded up into a ball of confusion in their minds. It made them *less* effective. It *decreased* rather than *increased* their sense of competence, self-confidence, and self-worth. They were getting the opposite result from the one they wanted. The products available to them were beyond useless. They were *anti-useful*. These people had "left brains" full of data. They couldn't get the data over into their right hemisphere so they could see what it meant. Therefore, they couldn't create a system of usable knowledge from it. They were still victims of normative systems—the problem they were trying to solve.

Our solution was to provide information as a system of knowledge they could assimilate and, therefore, use. We helped them create pictures of what the information *meant* in their minds' eyes.

Mastery Series was the name of the resulting product. It was a whole-brain learning system composed of videos and study books. Its specific purpose was to promote the Students' sense of personal achievement—of *being*. Each series was devoted to a particular species of gamefish in a certain type of water, such as stream fishing for trout or bass fishing in natural lakes.

The spiritual state of this system had been translated into material form. We had an exceptionally useful product for these particular users. Now we had to create a marketing system that linked the two. The number of potential users for each series was very small. Funds were tight. There was no room for waste, such as sending messages to non-prospects. Each series had to generate enough profit to support the launch of the next series. Stream Trout was the first series. To create a marketing plan that would generate the highest possible return on investment, our first question was, "Where *are* the Student Stream Trout fishermen?" We had to find a way to rank order U.S. geographic markets on the *density* of Student trout fisherman (Student trout fisherman per capita). By entering these markets first, we could make the launch almost self-funding. Because this task sounded nearly impossible, I asked Channing Stowell to do it. Chan probably understands the *essence* of database marketing better than anybody in the United States.

We had data. We knew household ownership of vcrs. We knew how many adults fly-fish. We had two proprietary studies among stream trout anglers. One showed the factors that discriminate Students from non-Students. The other indicated propensity to buy instructional videos.

Chan had to pull it all together so he could rank order 122 markets according to their relative return-on-marketing-investment potential. Our biggest worry was the sensitivity of the data. Only three million households in the U.S. contain someone who fly-fishes. Less than two million are Students. Could the data accurately rank 122 markets on something with less than 1 percent incidence in the population? To be useful, it had to. I held my breath.

Chan did it. When I saw the list, I finally exhaled. Here are the top six markets:

Market	% of U.S. Households	% of Total Prospects	Density Index
Casper-Riverton (Wyoming)	.04	0.81	2025
Cheyenne	.06	1.08	1800
Missoula-Butte (Montana)	.15	1.34	893
Boise	.18	1.21	672
Billings-Hardin (Montana)	.11	.66	600
Idaho Falls-Pocatello	.13	.75	576
Totals	.67	5.85	873 (avg. density index)

The list was face valid. These markets contain the great Western trout streams. Their incidence of Student trout anglers is nearly nine times greater than the national average. Chan's prioritization of markets, based only on data, followed the geographic presence of trout streams and trout fishing popularity across the United States.

Try something like this when you *haven't* championed the other principal complement of the system you're working in.

This is an example of designing one of the subsystems necessary to accomplish the business' originating purpose. It's the nature of jobs in open, adaptive systems. It provides the creative problem-solving challenges that make work life meaningful—and fun.

Sales and Distribution

Like marketing, sales is both a design and implementation function in an open, adaptive system. It must create plans that get the product to all those places where it interfaces with potential users. For example, the figure skating study found that aspiring competitors buy most of their equipment from independent skate shops. Most of these shops are in the same building as a skating rink, just as pro shops are often adjacent to golf courses. Even if the company already had distribution in chain sporting goods stores, located in high-traffic shopping areas, there's no reason to place this product in those stores. That's not where its potential users go to buy it.

Rather than put the product in outlets its prospective users don't frequent, the company must learn how to get the independent skate shop owners to not only carry it, but promote it. To do that, sales must conduct the same research of *the other*—in its case, the skate shop owners—that the use systems researchers conducted with skaters. What are the shop owners' goals? How do they achieve them? What works? What doesn't? The key question is, "How does this product help the shop owners achieve their goal?" The answer defines the most effective means of motivating them to stock and promote the product. It's a tool for them, just as it is for its users.

Of course this is just common sense. But it's common sense that a closed, normative company doesn't have. Trapped in form, it would place the product in chain sporting goods stores where it already has distribution because "that's the way we do things around here". Then it would wonder why the product didn't sell. Then it would increase advertising and promotion and chastise the sales force. That'd be effective.

Finance and Accounting

Open, adaptive businesses take the pain and guesswork out of Return On Investment. Financial reports become far more incisive tools for assessing performance. People in finance and accounting fund businesses and keep a financial scorecard on them. Therefore, they must be able to see the whole system and all its interconnecting parts. Normative business may have driven this function further off course than any other. It is entirely quantitative, focused on tracking and accounting for the money, rather than the operations of the business. In many companies, accrual accounting epitomizes the irrelevance Dawkins called "the overt error that is often fatal".

Activity Based Costing has already redesigned accounting to fit open, adaptive businesses. ABC tracks the activities of operations and then assigns costs to them. This provides process analyses. It challenges habituated practices. It points out possible waste. It builds up from specific processes to departmental functions to reflect the entire organization—a picture of the whole system painted in mathematics.

This is "systems accounting". It requires the same capacity to visualize systems required in the other functions. To realize its potential for operations analysis, it must be in the hands of someone who can see how the interaction of the organization's processes produce the scorecard—and, from that, identify opportunities to improve that are consistent with the businesses' purpose. Rather than simply controlling costs and tracking money, accounting can see where to spend money, why, and how much to spend, to make the whole system more functional.

Imagine never calling an accountant a "bean counter" again.

Summary

Open, adaptive, integrated businesses are simply organizations of people who think creatively, who originate actions and responses to achieve the system's purpose. Because the producer's people recognize *the other* principal complement, the users, and the purpose that unifies producer and users, these organizations continually regenerate themselves. They actively seek the puzzles and "felt tensions" that prevent entropy. This constant regeneration makes work life engaging, meaningful, fun. These organizations are the collective version of Joseph Campbell's "The essence of oneself and the essence of the world: these two are one."

An Integrative Person

An Integrative Business Organization

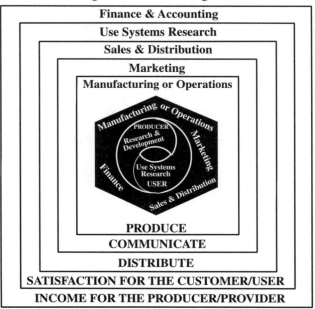

Life is not a comfortable settling down in pre-ordained grooves of being; at its best, it is elan vital, *inexorably driven toward a higher form of existence.... If life, after disturbance from outside, had simply returned to the so-called homeostatic equilibrium, it would never have progressed beyond the amoeba which, after all, is the best adapted creature in the world.*

—Ludwig von Bertalanffy, *General System Theory*

Chapter Ten
Our Hope for the Future

We may just be discovering systems, but we already have ample evidence that open systems work far more effectively than closed systems. How could that be? Simple. We just haven't recognized that the things that have worked better did so *because* they were open systems. And because we didn't know what we had, we allowed them to become closed, normative systems. Our hope for the future is to create and sustain our systems as open, integrative, and adaptive.

Democracy was founded as an open system. It has endured even though its original intention has been severely undermined by the extreme normalizing of both the Democratic and Republican parties. Today, the winner of any election is typically "the best horse in the glue factory". The election of Jesse Ventura as governor of Minnesota was an exception to that rule. That's why it got the attention of the entire country. Ventura is a throwback to democracy's original intent.

Education has created open systems to develop children's creative thinking abilities. Kids in traditional schools learn skills—reading, writing, and arithmatic—as rote processes they don't really understand. In open schools, they learn skills in the process of developing their ability to *think*, by creatively solving problems. I did a study of education several years ago. The difference between children in open and traditional curricula was striking.

One day I visited an open, fifth-grade class. One of the children spotted me at the doorway and walked over. "Hello, my name is Ray," he said. "Can I help you?"

"Yes," I replied, "I'm here to talk with your teacher about this kind of teaching."

"I'll introduce you," he said. He took me by the hand, led me to his teacher, and introduced us.

Then he directed my attention to small groups of kids scattered around the room. "See, we have teams of two or three kids all over. They're each working on their own projects. If you want to see what everybody is working on, I can take you around the class and tell you." I was stunned. This kid had more poise and self-confidence than most adults I've met. These teams were not isolated units. Each knew what the others were doing. As I looked around, I realized I was in a room full of kids learning both *how* and *why*. They were pursuing possibilities.

I visited a traditional fifth-grade class the next day. When I arrived in the classroom doorway, the students eyed me suspiciously. No one greeted me. They wouldn't even look at me directly. They just sat there, stooped over their desks. Their furtive glances said, "Now what trouble do you bring?" This was a room full of kids learning *how*, *when*, and *where* but not *why*. They were learning to avoid negative consequences.

Which ones do you think are going to find greater meaning and fulfillment in their lives?

In business, open systems are thoroughly proven although nearly unrecognized. The companies James Collins and Jerry Porras described as "visionary" in their book *Built to Last* at least *began* as open systems. Their philosophy rejected the normative definition of the purpose of business—"to make money". As Collins and Porras described it:

> Contrary to business school doctrine, *we did not find "maximizing shareholder wealth" or "profit maximization" as the dominant driving force or primary objective through the history of most of the visionary companies....*

PROFITABILITY is a necessary condition for existence and a means to more important ends, but it is not the end in itself for many of the visionary companies. Profit is like oxygen, food, water, and blood for the body; they are not the *point* of life, but without them, there is no life.

If profit wasn't *the point*, what was? Here's how some of the founders described it:

> *We try to remember that medicine is for the patient. We try never to forget that medicine is for the people. It is not for the profits. The profits follow, and if we have remembered that, they have never failed to appear. The better we have remembered it, the larger they have been.*
> —George Merck II, *Values and Visions:*
> *A Merck Century*

> *I don't believe we should make such an awful profit on our cars… I hold that it is better to sell a large number of cars at a reasonably small profit… I hold this because it enables a larger number of people to buy and enjoy the use of a car and because it gives a larger number of men employment at good wages.*
> —Henry Ford

> *You can look around* [in the general business world] *and still see people who are interested in money and nothing else, but the underlying drives come largely from a desire to do something else—to make a product—to give a service—generally to do something which is of value. So with that in mind, let us discuss why the Hewlett-Packard Company exists… The real reason for our existence is that we provide something which is unique* [that makes a contribution].
> —David Packard

> *We believe that our first responsibility is to the doctors, nurses, hospitals, mothers and all others who use our products.*
> —R.W. Johnson, Jr., the Johnson & Johnson *Credo*

The purpose of Motorola is to honorably serve the community by providing products and services of superior quality at a fair price to our customers; to do this so as to earn an profit which is required for the enterprise to grow, and by so doing provide the opportunity for our employees and shareholders to achieve their reasonable personal objectives.

—Paul Galvin, founder, Motorola

It's important to make people away from home feel that they're among friends and are really wanted.

—J. Willard Marriott, Sr.

Notice. These founding philosophies all acknowledge *the other*. These people recognized that business was about something more essential, more substantive, more meaningful than "making money". And most people treated them just as you'd expect. *Built to Last* gave an account of David Packard's encounter with the normative mind:

> [In 1949], I attended a meeting of business leaders. I suggested at the meeting that management people had a responsibility beyond that of making a profit for their stockholders. I said that we…had a responsibility to our employees to recognize their dignity as human beings, and to assure that they should share in the success which their work made possible. I pointed out, also, that we had a responsibility to our customers, and to the community at large, as well. I was surprised and shocked that not a single person at that meeting agreed with me. While they were reasonably polite in their disagreement, it was quite evident they firmly believed I was not one of them, and obviously not qualified to manage an important enterprise.

David Packard was one of Joseph Campbell's *Heroes*.

Even though money was not "the point", these companies have been disproportionately successful at making it. One dollar invested in a general stock market fund on January 1, 1926, would have grown to $415 by December 31, 1990. Collins and Porras directly compared the visionary companies to others in the same industries, of about the same age. That same dollar, invested in these comparison companies, would have been worth just over double the average of all companies by 1990— $955. But that dollar invested in the visionary companies would have grown to $6,356 in that period. And what is money? It's the reciprocal of usefulness received. These companies focused on the *cause* of the effect rather than the effect.

But there's even more evidence that these were open, integrative cultures—at least for some time. Collins and Porras noted their capacity for transcendent thinking. They called it, "No 'Tyranny of the OR' (embrace the 'Genius of the AND')." They described how visionary companies have the same comfort with paradox that creative people have. They called one element "Core Ideology" and the other "Drive for Progress". One "Core Ideology" item, for example, was "Has clear content". Opposite it, a "Drive for Progress" item was "Can be content-free". That appears paradoxical. Another pair was "Limits possibilities(to those consistent with the content of the ideology)" and "Expands the number and variety of possibilities (for accomplishing the core ideology)". That also appears paradoxical until you remember that one statement applies to *intent* and the other to the means of accomplishing it.

If "Core Ideology" were retitled "Purpose" and "Drive for Progress" were retitled "Processes", they'd describe an open system. "Core ideology" (purpose) remains constant. The forms and processes for achieving it change as necessary.

Did the people who started these companies do it this way because they consciously understood complex systems? Probably not. More likely, they took this approach because they were *original thinkers*. This made the most sense to them. However, I did find one instance of a company that was intentionally created to be an open, adaptive, integrative system by a man who understands complex systems.

Here are his founding principles for the company:

1. It must be equitably owned by all participants. No member should have preferential position. All advantage must result from individual ability and initiative.

2. It must be an enabling organization. No function should be performed by any part of the whole which could reasonably be done by a more peripheral part. Maximum power and freedom should be vested in the smallest, most peripheral parts, right on out to the individual.

3. It must be infinitely malleable yet extremely durable. It should be capable of constant, self-generated evolution of form or function without sacrificing its essential nature or embodied principle.

4. Governance must be distributive. No institution, no individual, and no combinations of either or both should be able to dominate discussion or control decisions.

5. It must embrace diversity and change. By that, it was meant that it must attract people and institutions which could become comfortable with such conditions and provide an environment in which they could flourish.

The man is Dee Hock. The business is VISA.

The organization that resulted from these principles is a community, which Hock described as "a concept to which people and resources are drawn in pursuit of a common purpose." This community, in 1998, had 23,000 member financial institutions in 200 countries, 600 million individual users who made 14 billion transactions that exceeded $1.2 trillion—the single largest block of consumer purchasing power in the world economy. But the organization Hock created didn't *make* this business successful—it *enabled* it to be successful.

What is a VISA card? It's a generic promissory note of value, just like cash or checks. But unlike cash, it's not a fixed denomination. Like a check, its denomination can be assigned at the time of the transaction. But unlike a check, the merchant is absolved from the risk of collecting unsecured debt. Merchants will accept it when they wouldn't accept a check. That, plus the time spread between taking possession of something and paying for it, allows buyers to make purchases they couldn't otherwise make. A VISA card is a more *useful* generic promissory note of value, to *both* principal complements of the business transaction, than either cash or checks, *provided* it is widely accepted. What did the VISA organization do? Well, the VISA card really is "everywhere", isn't it? There are many credit cards. Among themselves, they're commoditized. Any one does, or can do, what any other one does, pretty much the same way. How did VISA become so dominant? By knowing its purpose was to create wide availability. And to do that, it had to give up *control*. The financial institutions that create its products are, at one and the same time, its owners, members, and customers, its subjects, and superiors. VISA became the dominant credit card because the VISA organization was an open, adaptive *community*, focused on the core element of success. It vastly outperformed other organizations because it knew its true purpose and did whatever appropriate to accomplish it.

We also have many accounts of individual businesses that succeeded because they at least *began* as open systems. Here are descriptions of 3M's original successes from *Our Story—So Far—Notes from the First 75 Years of 3M Company*.

Francis G. Okie, a printing-ink maker and freelance inventor, created Wetordry sandpaper for 3M:

> 'We made printing ink on the second floor of an old building,' Okie was to say later. 'Our second-floor neighbor beveled glass for a living. He used a grinding wheel and there was considerable dust connected with the grinding. I often stopped in to visit with him, and one day he mentioned something about wanting to get out of the glass-beveling business. I wondered why.
>
> 'But as I watched him working, I noticed the dust he had to breathe and realized that this probably had something to do with his wanting to sell. After talking with him, I began to wonder why a person couldn't make a waterproof abrasive, a sandpaper that could be used with water. This would eliminate the dust from abrading.
>
> 'I decided to experiment. I had to find out if there was such a thing as waterproof sandpaper on the market. I went to one of the oldest varnish makers in America—they were sandpaper jobbers as well—and asked to buy waterproof sandpaper. The clerk said there was no such thing.
>
> 'Then I went to work. I bought small packages of mineral. I mixed the adhesive, spread it by hand onto paper backing, and sprinkled garnet on it. I had my neighbor, the glass-beveler, try it. I also tested it by sanding boards in my own shop.
>
> 'When I was convinced I had something, I went to a competitor of 3M's, and asked them to make a trial run of sandpaper for me using my bonding agent. They agreed. The sandpaper they turned out further convinced me I had a salable product. Funny thing, they never asked me why I wanted the sandpaper or what I was doing with it. Then I got some people interested in backing me and when I couldn't get any mineral in the east, I wrote Minnesota Mining.'

Mr. Okie and 3M formed an exclusive working relationship. He developed a product that worked. Notice where he began—his frequent visits to his neighbor's shop, his investigation of the glass-beveler's desire to get out of the business. That's *use systems research*. It identified a problem he felt was worth solving.

Shortly after the product was developed, 3M found another market for it. 3M was calling on auto manufacturers and automotive body shops at the time Wetordry was introduced. Its salespeople saw the product's superior usefulness for these potential customers:

> One of 3M's eastern salesmen, Joseph C. Duke, later a company director, made the first call on an auto paint shop. Duke found the auto painter using the traditional pumice to rub down the car. He wasn't receptive to a demonstration of waterproof sandpaper. ('The sand will come off,' the painter insisted.) He admitted pumice got into the crevices of the car and had to be scraped out and that the pumice sometimes cut deeper into the surface than he wanted it to.

> But he finally agreed to a demonstration and when Duke finished sanding the surface, the painter's response was immediate. 'Come here!' he yelled to his helper. 'This man's got something.' The painter was so excited about 'Wetordry' sandpaper that he placed an order on the spot and told Duke the product would sell to every car painter in Philadelphia.

> 'We grabbed a phone book,' Duke said later, 'found a whole slew of painters to call on and, as the man said, each placed an order. 3M was soon calling on shops all over the country.

> At the same time, salesmen were persuading more automobile makers that 3M had the answer to their finishing problems. Waterproof sandpaper could be used with either water or oil, which cut down the friction heat and allowed workmen to produce a smoother finish on the new cars. It also cut faster under lubrication than dry sandpaper.

> With the newly developed lacquer and the novel sanding system, an auto body could be completed in three or four days instead of requiring weeks of work as before.

What did Joseph Duke do? He identified a specific problem with pumice that Wetordry could solve. More important, he provided a tool that championed its user. "An auto body could be completed in three or four days instead of requiring weeks of work as before." That's "competitively superior usefulness".

Our Story—So Far also describes how masking tape and Scotch™ cellophane tape came about. Masking tape was specifically developed to solve a problem with masking cars for two-tone paint jobs. The body shops used newspapers, butcher paper, improvised glues, and surgical adhesive tape to mask parts of the car body. Ripping off the mask often ruined the new paint job. 3M created a new adhesive and backing to solve that problem—masking tape.

Companies were asking 3M for help in packaging their products. Packaging perishable foods in cellophane was particularly difficult. 3M developed Scotch™ Tape by applying the adhesive expertise it gained from the masking tape experience to a different substrate—cellophane. The originating purpose of Scotch™ Tape was to package perishable foods more effectively.

These three products were founding flagships of the company. They all began as systems that recognized both principal complements, whose purpose was to solve *the other's* problem and help that *other* achieve his or her goal. These products championed *the other*. Those *others* became loyal users.

Once in a while, 3M still listens to *the other*. Here's a business that would never have been successfully commercialized if it hadn't.

I started doing use systems research for 3M's Commercial Tape Division in 1976. My client was Bill Schoonenberg, the division's director of Market Information Services, which included market research. He'd hired me to find out if several proposed new products would be viable businesses. I shot down the first six because I couldn't find any potential use systems in which they were uniquely useful. Those were the experiences that showed me how thoroughly 3M embraced the "trial and error" approach to new business development.

One day Bill asked, "Do you think you can figure out if this thing is a business or not? I'm sick of it circling. We should either launch it or kill it, but I want to know why, in either case."

This adhesive had been kicking around 3M for about nine years. People called it "a failed adhesive experiment." It was still alive because Art Fry, in R&D, wouldn't let it die. Art believed there was something there. But what?

I reviewed the applications Art had tried. The common denominator was that they were all paper products. Since the division's general market was offices, my first question was, "What paper, in offices, do people attach, to anything, and how do they perceive those jobs?" I developed a list—notes on letters and reports, telephone messages, reference markers on books and periodicals, blocking out sections of documents before duplicating, etcetera.

Then I interviewed people who performed these tasks. I discovered that attaching two pieces of paper was so menial that people didn't think about it and couldn't discuss it. Yet people inside 3M who had used the product were actually gleeful about it. The only way to get at the product's viability was to explore what people actually did with it and how they felt about it—behaviors and emotions, not intellectualizations.

We made up product samples for the hypothesized uses, gave them to potential users, asked them to record their use daily over a two-week period, and then interviewed them. We gave book markers to librarians. We gave secretaries the note version and versions for blocking out portions of documents. We gave art studios colored paper for layouts. In all, we had nine different product forms. Here's what we found:

1. Everybody, regardless of specific use, was enthusiastic;

2. For some applications, such as book markers that stayed in place but didn't tear the page when removed, the unique usefulness was obvious. For the note version, it wasn't. People still couldn't explain their enthusiasm;

3. The longer people played with the note version, the more places they stuck it. The product was addictive.

My conclusions were:

1. The product was definitely a viable business;

2. Sampling was the *only* way to generate adoption. People would not seriously consider the product intellectually. They had a positive emo-

tional reaction only *after* using it. Prior to that, it appeared too inconsequential to deserve their attention.

Bill ran some quantitative studies to determine the volume and profit potential of the different product versions, selected the note form, and introduced it into four test markets. Less than a year later, he called. "Hey, you @##&**@!!!!!," he said. "You told us this was a real business. We've got Post-It™ Notes in four test markets, and we can't give 'em away."

"Speaking of giving them away, have you?" I asked.

"No, we can't," he replied. "There's a company policy against giving free goods with a new product introduction."

I replied, "Look, you give 'em away, you have a business. You don't, you don't. That's it. Those are your only options."

Bill acknowledged what we knew about prospective users and responded accordingly. He side-stepped the corporate policy by opening a fifth test market as a "promotion test." There, he sampled Post-It™ Notes, proved out the business, and forced success on a company that was sufficiently normalized to prevent it.

Bill worked as an open system inside a closed system. That can be hazardous to a person's career. He made the business happen and got away with it largely, I believe, because 3M still had, from its origins, greater respect for open-system traits than most companies.

Some companies have none, and the hero gets sacrificed, even though the business is wildly successful. At one time, consumers could hardly tell the difference between the crust of a frozen pizza and the cardboard plate beneath it. Joe Burke, the new business development manager of Pillsbury's Frozen Foods Division, Totino's, identified the problem. R&D, with its extensive dough technology, developed a crust that consumers recognized as superior to other frozen pizza crusts. While manufacturing was gearing up, Joe spent his days preventing top management from screwing up the opportunity. His definitive victory came when he convinced them not to remove reference to "competitors' cardboard crusts" from the introductory ad campaign. Why did they want to do that? They didn't want to "offend competition".

The product would never have made it had Joe not known that *more useful*, to frozen pizza users, meant "a crust like pizzeria pizza, not cardboard". Even if it had been commercialized, its advertising would have been meaningless to potential users. As it turned out, Totino's went from the No. 2 brand in 60 percent of the country to the No. 1 brand in 100 percent of the country. Joe won the battle, but management won the war. He left the company.

Many successful entrepreneurs began their businesses as open systems, grounded in inherent understanding of *the other*—because *the other* was originally *themselves*. They were people highly dissatisfied with the tool they had for their job. They were the people with the problem. They knew the use system intimately. They knew their goal, their processes for achieving it, what worked, what didn't. They knew precisely what *more useful* meant. Unable to find a satisfactory tool, they invented one. They were reincarnations of the original toolmaker. Selling the more useful tool to others who had the same problem created profitable businesses. Their problem, not its solution, was the origin of their success.

We have plenty of evidence that the open-system approach to creating human social systems produces spectacular results. We also have plenty of evidence that such systems don't remain open. In other words, they aren't ongoing open, *adaptive* systems.

In 1965 IBM was trying to gain market acceptance of the 360 mainframe. Its pinstripers didn't sell computers. They sold what the computer could do to solve its users' problems. They deliberately investigated customer problems. They used IBM's capabilities to solve it. At the time, they didn't separate hardware from software. Both were necessary to solve the problem. This produced IBM's original success.

That changed in the early 1970s, when "plug-compatible" competitors such as Amdahl positioned their products strictly on price. "Our box can do everything their box can do, and it's cheaper," Amdahl claimed. And IBM fell for it. Forgetting why it succeeded in the first place, IBM focused on product and price instead of usefulness. It saw competitors instead of users. It unbundled software and hardware, breaking a whole problem-solving system into pieces. It started telling customers what they were going to get. "We'll give you a fancier, bigger, longer-lasting box." IBM changed from open, adaptive, and integrative to the archetype of a closed, normative system. The company became so isolated I once remarked that the only major move still available to it was to secede from the Union.

In its glory days, Procter and Gamble used the open system approach to creating new businesses. It investigated dissatisfactions among users of specific types of products to find new business opportunities. The company would identify a large, growing category in grocery stores and find out how users felt about those products. When it found substantial dissatisfaction, P&G would develop a new tool that better suited the user's purpose.

When P&G asked consumers to describe the primary goal of caring for their teeth, one large group said, "to prevent cavities". Another said, "To keep my teeth white and bright". P&G asked both groups how satisfied they were. Neither was. Crest toothpaste was P&G's more useful tool for those whose primary goal was to prevent cavities. Gleem toothpaste was how it helped those who wanted brighter, whiter teeth achieve their goal.

I have used several examples throughout this book to illustrate that 3M is a closed culture even though, as you have seen, its original success was based on intimate understanding of the other principal complement. Hewlett-Packard recently completed a major "growth initiative". Its purpose was "to find ways to sustain our annual compound growth rate of 20 percent". That sure looks like a "maximize shareholder profits" motivation. Perhaps David Packard really is gone.

I searched *Built to Last* for indications that at least some visionary companies had sustained their open-system origins. I didn't find them. What I found was Chapter Six, entitled "Cult-like Cultures". That's not encouraging. It portrays intense indoctrination of the employee into the company's philosophy, great emphasis on the fit between the employee and the culture. It talked about on-the-job socialization, exposure to pervasive mythology of heroic deeds and corporate exemplars, unique "in" language and terminology, corporate songs and cheers, celebrations that reinforce belonging, plant and office layouts that reinforce norms and ideals, constant verbal and written emphasis on corporate values, heritage and the sense of being part of something special, incentive and advancement criteria explicitly linked to the person's fit with corporate ideology. In spite of some emphasis on ideology, there's much more stress on form and process. I had to conclude that these cultures became normative. There's too much emphasis on imitation—planting memes in employees' minds—for me to think otherwise. The irony is that it appears these companies are conditioning their employees to a *specific* open, integrative philosophy rather than developing their ability to *be* open and adaptive.

Why do companies that once apparently "got it" no longer "get it"?

Because, except for Dee Hock and VISA, they didn't know what "it" is. The founders of these companies probably did not have a frame of reference for systems. They weren't aware of the natural principles behind their philosophy. They simply considered it "common sense." They also recognized they lived in a world where "common sense" was so uncommon they felt compelled to force it on the culture.

What if they had understood open, integrative systems? They would also have recognized the nature of the employee pool. The vast majority of adults in the U.S. are highly normalized, linear thinkers by the time they leave grade school, let alone by the time they go to work. Even if the founders of these companies did understand the principles behind their success, how could they perpetuate them? Could they trust people trained not to think creatively, not to ask "why?" to keep creating new realities guided only by the organization's core purpose? Obviously, they couldn't.

Dee Hock recognized this problem. He said:

> There were weaknesses in VISA' s execution of the concept, as well as external conditions it could not overcome.

Of the core VISA organization, he said:

> There existed no pool of potential employees familiar with Chaordic concepts and no place where they could be educated.

(*Chaord* is a word Hock coined to mean "any self-organizing, adaptive, nonlinear, complex system, whether physical, biological or social, the behavior of which exhibits characteristics of both chaos and order." Hock's view of knowledge is that it lies on the border between chaos and order. Chaord, therefore, means an open, integrative system that constantly learns in order to adapt.)

Of the network of financial institutions that distribute VISA's products, he said:

> Although the core and concept of VISA were Chaordic, members remained mechanistic and linear, without ability to fully exploit the concept and with continual inclination to reimpose archaic structure and management practices on the organization.

Of the external normative institutions VISA encountered, he said:

> Commercial law did not anticipate, thus could not prevent but did not fit the concept. Like a dead tree falling on a sapling, the law continually warped and constricted the natural evolution of the organization in ways beyond correction.

About the overall effect of imposing closed, normative thinking on this open system he said:

> Had those three constraints alone not existed, the VISA community could easily be quadruple its present dimensions. By the turn of the century such restraints will scarcely exist. The opportunity for Chaordic organization continues to beggar the imagination.

When you recognize what VISA accomplished *in spite of* normative constraints, you get some feeling for the intrinsic power of open, integrative systems compared to closed, normative ones.

It's unfortunate that the opportunity to champion *the others'* pursuit of their self-actualization—and, in the process, champion our own "rapture of being alive"—has not been a real opportunity until we began to recognize the nature of systems and, specifically, the difference between formative, normative, and integrative phases. But now that we have done that, it is. And there's no confusion about the element most critical to realizing it—people.

Integrative social systems are simply communities of integrative people. Chapter Nine described a group of integrative people in a business community. Integrative parents produce integrative children. Integrative teachers produce integrative students. Integrative elected officials govern in the best interests of the citizens.

The lives of integrative people are rich in meaning. Integrative people create environments that support others in their pursuit of meaning. This is the means by which the whole world comes together someplace. That's our hope for the future.

The essence of oneself and the essence of the world: these two are one.... The aim is not to see, [although that is a prerequisite step] but to realize that one is, that essence; then one is free to wander as that essence in the world.

—Joseph Campbell, *The Power of Myth*
with Bill Moyers

Conclusion

Converting human social systems to open, adaptive, integrative systems permits people both to satisfy their material needs *and* have meaning in their lives. That conversion begins with us, individually—systems of one.

Most people must first overcome the way they've been conditioned to think. Then, when they can see the intangible dynamics that cause the material effects, the fun really starts. They must overcome the threats and punishments of the normative systems that surround them. This, as Joseph Campbell put it, is "the hero's journey". To take it, keep asking "Why?" until you get an answer that causes you to say Aha!

Csikszentmihalyi put it this way:

> The answer to the old riddle "What is the meaning of life?" turns out to be astonishingly simple. The meaning of life is meaning; whatever it is, wherever it comes from, a unified purpose is what gives meaning to life.

The reward for making the journey is a life that has meaning, a life of freedom or, in Campbell's words, "the rapture of being alive".

Often, people who have successfully negotiated this journey are viewed as mystics. If a person who can see obvious, self-evident truths that simply have no material form defines a mystic, then they are mystics. But then so could we all be.

To Contact Cliff Havener

If you have any questions or would like to comment on
Meaning—The Secret of Being Alive, contact
Cliff Havener via e-mail.
Go to http://www.forseekers.com

Bibliography

Vitalism and Mechanism A Discussion between Herbert V. Neal, Ph.D., Sc.D. Professor of Zoology and Dean in Tufts College and James F. Porter. Lancaster, PA: The Science Press Printing Company, 1934.

Adams, Scott. *The Dilbert Principle.* New York: HarperBusiness, 1996.

Ashworth, William. *The Economy of Nature.* Boston, MA: Houghton-Mifflin, 1995.

Bach, Richard. *Illusions: The Adventures of a Reluctant Messiah.* New York: Dell Publishing, 1977.

Briggs, John, and Peat, F. David. *The Turbulent Mirror.* New York: Harper Row, 1989.

Campbell, Joseph. *Hero with a Thousand Faces.* Princeton, NJ: Princeton University Press, First Edition, 1949, Second Edition, 1968.

Campbell, Joseph, and Moyers, Bill. *The Power of Myth.* New York: Doubleday, 1988.

Capra, Fritjof. *The Turning Point.* New York: Simon & Schuster, 1982.

Collins, James C., and Porras, Jerry I. *Built to Last.* New York: Harper Business, 1994.

Csikszentmihalyi, Mihaly. *Flow: The Psychology of Optimal Experience.* Harper Perennial, 1991.

Csikszentmihalyi, Mihaly. *Creativity: Flow and the Psychology of Discovery and Invention.* Harper Perennial, 1997.

Dawkins, Richard. *The Selfish Gene.* New York: Oxford University Press, 1989.

De Geus, Arie. *The Living Company.* Boston: Harvard Business School Press, 1997.

Driesch, Hans. *The History and Theory of Vitalism.* London: Authorized Translation by C.K. Ogden. MacMillan and Co. Limited, 1914.

Ferguson, Marilyn. *The Aquarian Conspiracy.* Los Angeles, CA: J.P. Tarcher, Inc., 1980.

Frankl, Viktor E., *Man's Search for Meaning.* Boston: Beacon Press, 1992.

Galbraith, John Kenneth. *Economics In Perspective: A Critical History.* Boston: Houghton Mifflin Company, 1987.

Gaukroger, Stephen. *Descartes: An Intellectual Biography.* Oxford: Clarendon Press, 1995.

Gibran, Kahlil. *The Prophet.* New York: Alfred A. Knopf, Inc., 1966.

Gleick, James. *Chaos.* New York: Viking Press, 1987.

Greenough, Horatio. *Form and Function.* Berkeley, CA: University of California Press, 1947.

Hagberg, Janet. *Real Power.* Minneapolis, MN: Winston Press, 1984.

Hale, Jonathan. *The Old Way of Seeing.* Boston, MA: Houghton-Mifflin, 1994.

Harris, Thomas Anthony. *I'm OK, You're OK: A practical guide to transactional analysis.* New York: Harper Publishing, 1969.

Heinlein, Robert. *Stranger in a Strange Land.* New York: G. P. Putnam's Sons, 1991.

Hock, Dee. *Institutions in the Age of Mindcrafting.* Unpublished paper presented at: Self-Organizing Systems: The New Science of Change, Park City, UT, 1994.

Infeld, Leopold. *Albert Einstein: His Work and its Influence on our World*. New York: Charles Scribner's Sons, 1950.

Keeney, Bradford. *Shaking Out the Spirits*. Barrytown, NY: Station Hill Press Inc., 1994.

Kuhn, Thomas. *The Structure of Scientific Revolutions*. Chicago, Il: University of Chicago Press, 1970.

Land, George, and Jarman, Beth. *Breakpoint and Beyond*. New York: Harper Business, 1992.

Langer, Ellen J. *Mindfulness*. Reading, MA: Addison-Wesley Publishing Company, 1990.

Leider, Dick. *The Power of Purpose*. San Francisco, CA: Berrett-Kehler, 1997.

Maslow, Abraham H. *Motivation and Personality*. New York: Harper Publishing, 1954.

Miller, Perry. *Errand Into the Wilderness*. Boston, MA: Harvard University Press, 1956.

Mitchell, Arnold. *The Nine American Lifestyles: who we are and where we're going*. New York, Macmillian Publishing, 1983.

Notestein, Wallace. *The English People on the Eve of Colinization*. New York: Harper and Row, 1954.

Powell, John. *Fully Human, Fully Alive*. Niles, IL: Argus Communication, 1976.

Samuels, Mike, M.D., and Samuels, Nancy. *Seeing with the Mind's Eye: The History, Techniques and Uses of Visualization*. Co-published by Random House, Inc. New York, N.Y. and The Bookworks, La Jolla, California

Smolin, Lee. *Life of the Cosmos*. New York: Oxford University Press, 1997.

3M Company. *Our Story So Far*. Saint Paul, MN: Minnesota Mining and Manufacturing Company, 1977.

Torrance, E. Paul. *Guiding Creative Talent*. Englewood Cliffs, N.J.: Prentice-Hall Inc., 1962.

Torrance, E. Paul. *Why Fly? A Philosophy of Creativity*. Norwood, NJ: Ablex Publishing Corporation, 1995.

Torrance, E. Paul. *Education and the Creative Potential*. Minneapolis: University of Minnesota Press, 1963.

Tzu, Lao. *Tao Teh King*. Interpreted as *Nature and Intelligence*. Archie J. Bahm. Albuquerque, NM: World Books, 1986.

von Bertalanffy, Ludwig. *General System Theory*. New York: George Braziller Inc., 1968.

von Bertalanffy, Ludwig. *Robots, Men and Minds: Psychology in the Modem World*. New York: George Braziller, 1967.

Waters, Frank. *Book of the Hopi*. New York: Penguin Books, 1977.

Wheatley, Margaret J. *Leadership and the New Science*. San Francisco, CA: Berrett-Kehler publishers, 1992.

Williams, William Appleman. *The Contours of American History*. Chicago: Quadrangle Books, 1966.